THE
IVP POCKET REFERENCE
SERIES

POCKET DICTIONARY OF

CHRISTIAN
SPIRITUALITY

Over 300 terms clearly
and concisely defined

DON THORSEN

IVP Academic

An imprint of InterVarsity Press
Downers Grove, Illinois

InterVarsity Press
P.O. Box 1400, Downers Grove, IL 60515-1426
ivpress.com
email@ivpress.com

InterVarsity Press® is the book-publishing division of InterVarsity Christian Fellowship/ USA®, a movement of students and faculty active on campus at hundreds of universities, colleges, and schools of nursing in the United States of America, and a member movement of the International Fellowship of Evangelical Students. For information about local and regional activities, visit intervarsity.org.

Design: Cindy Kiple

ISBN 978-0-8308-4967-3 (print)
ISBN 978-0-8308-8732-3 (digital)

Printed in the United States of America ∞

InterVarsity Press is committed to ecological stewardship and to the conservation of natural resources in all our operations. This book was printed using sustainably sourced paper.

Library of Congress Cataloging-in-Publication Data

A catalog record for this book is available from the Library of Congress.

P 20 19 18 17 16 15 14 13 12 11 10 9 8 7 6 5 4 3 2 1

Y 35 34 33 32 31 30 29 28 27 26 25 24 23 22 21 20 19 18

To my daughter
Dana Thorsen
who is an inspiration and
encouragement to me
as well as to others.

CONTENTS

Preface

Spirituality has to do with the human spirit, and Christian spirituality has to do with our relationship with the divine Spirit—with God. In particular, Christian spirituality has to do with our relationship with God, who in Scripture is revealed as our heavenly Father, as *Abba*—a term of personal intimacy—by Jesus Christ. Jesus atoned for people's salvation from sin and judgment through his life, death, and resurrection. Through him people are saved and are reconciled to God by grace through faith. However, the story of salvation does not end with conversion and the hope of eternal life. Jesus promised that the Holy Spirit would continue to work in and through the lives of believers—of Christians—in healing, restoring, and transforming them spiritually and holistically. Salvation is as much for this life as for life hereafter as God's Spirit works sanctifying grace in the lives of believers. In Scripture as well as church history, many activities, exercises, and disciplines of spiritual import have been practiced. God graciously intends for them to serve as a means by which believers may grow in faith, hope, and love; in intimacy in their personal relationship with God; and in their obedient maturation into Christlikeness.

One should beware of having an exclusively spiritualistic understanding of Christian spirituality. On the contrary, Christian spirituality ought to be thought of as something that is holistic, embracing all aspects of life: spiritual and physical, supernatural and natural, individual and social, gift and task, justification and sanctification, love and justice, scriptural and traditional, rational and experiential, sacramental and symbolic, extemporaneous and disciplined, and so on. The study of Christian spirituality is not intended to limit but to expand on its holistic relevance to people here and now.

The *Pocket Dictionary of Christian Spirituality* is my contribution to the InterVarsity Press reference series of pocket dictionaries. Certainly these topics are just as important to Christians as the information found in the other pocket dictionaries. Because this book is a part of a reference series, it will be more descriptive than prescriptive with regard to defining spiritual formation and Christian living.

Because of the varieties of Christian spirituality, it is difficult to present evenhandedly all the beliefs, values, and practices of each church tradition—east and west; north and south; liturgical and evangelical; Catholic, Orthodox, and Protestant. Because of the genre of the *Pocket Dictionary of Christian Spirituality*, terms have been defined simply, but not simplistically. If you want to learn more about specific beliefs, values, and practices related to Christian spirituality, then investigate them further as a spiritual study for yourself.

Let me give one example of differences among Christians with regard to spirituality. It has to do with the degree to which Christian spirituality (including its growth and formation) is considered a divine gift, and the degree to which it is considered a human responsibility or task. For example, in 1 Corinthians 3:6, the apostle Paul says, "I planted, Apollos watered, but God gave the growth." Christians believe that God alone provides the salvation and spiritual growth people experience. However, they disagree with regard to the degree to which people have the responsibility or task of "abiding" in Jesus Christ, cooperating with God's Holy Spirit for their salvation and spiritual growth (see John 15:1-11). What does it mean for Paul to "plant" and for Apollos to "water"? What do these words of Scripture mean for us today for our role in salvation and for our spiritual growth?

In answering these questions, some Christians emphasize how God sovereignly decrees all matters related to salvation and spiritual growth. At most, people are thought to act compatibly with God's grace, but in no way do they work for or merit their salvation and spiritual growth. Other Christians, while they agree that they cannot work for or merit their salvation and spiritual growth, emphasize that God self-limits divine power over people, and preveniently gives them grace to decide—accepting or rejecting—God's salvation and aid for spiritual growth.

On the one hand, those who emphasize God's sovereign decrees may understand the definitions in this *Pocket Dictionary of Christian Spirituality* as descriptions of the effectual outworkings of God's plan for their lives. On the other hand, those who emphasize God's prevenient grace may understand the definitions as imperatives for synergistically cooperating with the Holy Spirit for their spiritual formation.

Both views believe that some degree of divine gift and human task is at work for people's salvation and for their spiritual growth, despite differences with regard to the extent of their respective roles for people's spiritual well-being, discipleship, and formation. As you read the *Pocket Dictionary of Christian Spirituality*, some definitions may seem to place greater emphasis on the role of God in people's salvation and spiritual growth. Others may seem to place greater emphasis on God's expectation that people act responsibly—aided by divine grace—in "planting" and "watering" for their salvific and spiritual well-being. All definitions affirm that it is God alone who gives the growth.

Acknowledgments

I want to thank Steve Wilkens for advising me to write the *Pocket Dictionary of Christian Spirituality* and for his ongoing friendship and collegiality. I also want to thank Dan Reid for his editorial expertise and for patiently working with me on the dictionary. Special thanks go to Jini Kilgore Cockroft and Rebecca Russo for reading and commenting on my final manuscript. Jared Bjur provided invaluable help as my research assistant, and I am especially grateful to him. Others who gave input to the *Pocket Dictionary of Christian Spirituality* include Kyle Fraser, Brian Eager, Jake Evers, Dan Lane, and Dan Tkach.

As always, I am thankful to my daughters Liesl and Dana Thorsen, and to Heidi and her husband Will Oxford, for their ongoing love and support of my writing habit, which for me is a spiritual discipline. In particular, I want to honor my daughter Dana, to whom this book is dedicated. Dana, blessings!

Biblical References and Abbreviations

All references to Scripture come from the New Revised Standard Version (NRSV), unless otherwise stated. They are used to illustrate the scriptural roots of beliefs, values, and practices related to Christian spirituality, rather than act as proofs of them.

The Hebrew Scriptures, known by Christians as the Old Testament, will be abbreviated as OT. The Christian Scriptures, known by Christians as the New Testament, will be abbreviated as NT.

In talking about spiritual formation, some foreign phrases (ancient and modern) are commonly used. In these references, abbreviations to other languages are as follows:

Aram. = Aramaic
Ger. = German
Gk. = Greek
Heb. = Hebrew
Kor. = Korean
Lat. = Latin
Old Eng. = Old English

A

abandonment, spiritual. A *detachment from the anxieties of the world and entrusting oneself wholly to God for the sake of spiritual *contemplation. Related terms include the renunciation of self-centeredness and disinterested *love for God, advocated for example, by seventeenth- and eighteenth-century French *quietists.

Abba **(Aram., "father").** The intimate term for one's father that *Jesus Christ used for God. Although Jesus also used the Greek word *pater* to refer to his Father, the occasional appearance of this Aramaic word (transliterated into Greek) suggests it was his way of addressing God. The intimacy is thought to communicate a deeper, more filial relationship between ourselves and God. Later NT Christians also referred to God as *Abba*, showing that we may have the same kind of relationship with God as did Jesus (e.g., Romans 8:15). Spiritually, *Abba* helps Christians today to pursue God in a way that is filial, relational, and intimate.

abiding in Christ. Living in ways that acknowledge that *Jesus Christ is our source of spiritual power (John 15:4); Christians participate "*in Christ" (2 Corinthians 5:17), through the presence and power of the Holy *Spirit, and follow his teachings (1 John 2:27). Christians use the phrase to describe the proper place they should be spiritually in relationship with Jesus, both for their *salvation and spiritual growth.

absolution. The proclamation—for example, by a Roman Catholic or Orthodox priest—that the sins of a penitent have been forgiven by God after they have been *confessed and repented. Based on Matthew 18:18, a priest may choose to withhold absolution until a *penance (discipline) is completed, especially in cases of grave sin.

activist spirituality. A type of spirituality that emphasizes compassion and advocacy on behalf of those who are impoverished or unjustly treated, spiritually as in other ways—culturally, financially, and politically. Participation in compassion ministries and social activism is considered a heightened expression of Christian spirituality. Concerns of activist spirituality include advocacy for the poor, who have been ignored, marginalized, oppressed, and persecuted (*see* liberation).

ACTS (prayer). An acrostic guide to prayer used as a mnemonic device for adoration, confession, thanksgiving, and supplication.

administration, gift of. A special enabling of the Holy *Spirit that empowers believers for spiritual or church leadership, such as for vision casting and managing others.

adoration. Expression of affection, admiration, and love, especially toward God. Adoration is an important part of *praising God in *prayer and other aspects of one's relationship with God.

Advent. The "coming" (Lat., *adventus*; cf. Gk., *parousia*) of *Jesus Christ, especially in reference to his birth. Nowadays Advent primarily refers to the beginning of the Christian church year (*see* calendar, Christian), and the four Sundays preceding it (*see* Christmas). The Advent may also refer to Jesus' second coming.

affection. A human emotion or desire; it may have to do with a liking for someone or something. The spiritual dimension of human experience has sometimes been described as the religious affections. Historically, Christians have been wary of religious affections, considering them to be secondary—even disrupting—to Christian faith, hope, and love (*see* virtues, theological). Be that as it may, there is thought to be an interconnectedness between human and religious affections. According to Jonathan Edwards, proper religious affections, as typified by the *fruit of the Spirit, moderate the extremes of Christian intellectualism and emotionalism.

agapē. A Greek word for *love, thought to be the highest form of unconditional, self-giving love. Although various Greek words are translated in Scripture as "love," *agapē* was used most often to describe God's love for people, and the kind of love people are to have for God and for others. Throughout church history, *agapē* has been the goal of perfect love for which Christians have aspired in their spiritual pursuit of *holiness.

amen. A Hebrew word of acclamation, meaning "so be it" or "let it be." Both Jews and Christians use *amen* in *prayer and *liturgy as a response to religious affirmations, *thanksgivings, and *benedictions (e.g., 2 Corinthians 1:20). In some translations of *Scripture, *amen* is translated as "verily" or "truly" (e.g., John 5:24). Spiritually, *amen* is used as a solemn and fervent conclusion to people's prayers, individually or collectively.

amulet. An item of religious significance, often worn around the neck or on other parts of the body. The Jews wore phylacteries, which were receptacles that usually contained scriptural texts. Later, Christians wore religious jewelry as simple as a *cross or crucifix, or as complex as a locket containing a holy relic. Amulets serve to remind people of God and matters related to God, or serve as a witness to others.

angels. Heavenly beings, created by God, who serve as celestial messengers and servants of God. Angels aid people for salvation and also for their *spiritual formation, sometimes described as ministering angels (see Hebrews 1:14). Some Christians consider angels to be guardians of individuals, or of entire groups, cities, and regions, and believe they engage in *spiritual warfare with *demons.

antinomianism. The belief that Christians are not bound by *laws, but are morally free due to *grace. The term *antinomianism* combines Greek words that mean "against" (*anti*) and "law" (*nomos*). This belief asserts that Christians are exempt from the moral teachings of *Scripture, including those of *Jesus Christ. Most Christians have been as critical of antinomianism as its opposite: works righteousness. Although Christians are saved by grace through *faith, they are not exempt from God's *holiness and justice, and Christlike living.

apologetic spirituality. *See* studious spirituality.

apostleship, gift of. A special enabling of the Holy *Spirit that empowers believers for spreading the *gospel, especially in new ways or areas. The original disciples were called apostles. So also was Paul and some others (e.g., Andronicus, Junia). Some Christians believe in a limited and authoritative view of apostolicity that ceased in biblical times, whereas other Christians believe that God continues to enable apostles today. *See also* gifts of the Holy Spirit.

arts. Various arts, *music, and *dance used for promoting spirituality and worship. Historically, *icons have been important artistic expressions of Christianity. Spirituality and *worship take many forms, and the arts can creatively contribute to their development through engaging multiple senses in celebration of and meditation on God.

asceticism. The practice of self-denial. Asceticism consists of extreme self-discipline for the sake of spiritual *purification, insight, and pursuit of other practices that enable Christians to abstain from physical and earthly concerns. Ascetics practice physical ascesis (i.e., self-denial) in aid of mental and spiritual ascesis, leading to tranquility as well as to *union (or communion) with God. Asceticism may be individual or collective. In the ancient church, there were various ways that Christians took "flight from the world" (Lat., *fuga mundi*). For example, *martyrs were viewed as those who most exemplified *fuga mundi*. After Constantine, *fuga mundi* expanded into communal withdrawal from the world, resulting in various *monastic movements.

ashram, Christian. Originally a monastic dwelling for Hindus. Catholic and Indian converts adopted them in emphasizing a similar lifestyle defined by external quiet, *simplicity, *meditation, and *worship. Christian ashrams—both Catholic and Protestant—became places of spiritual *retreat, or sometimes small communities in which members contribute to one another's needs.

assurance of salvation. The confidence people have of their *salvation, attested to by God and other evidences. *Scripture promises that those who *repent and believe will receive eternal life; Scripture also says that the Holy *Spirit bears "witness with our spirit that we are children of God" (Romans 8:16). These assurances, along with other evidences that occur in the lives of believers, contribute to the confidence they may have for salvation—for example, "peace of God" (Philippians 4:7) and "*fruit of the Spirit" (Galatians 5:22-23). The assurance of salvation frees Christians to focus more on *spiritual formation and in expressing love to God and others. *See also* perseverance of the saints.

Augustinianism. The theology of Augustine of Hippo (354–430), which distinctively emphasizes the sovereignty of God, human depravity, and God's unconditional decree of *salvation. In the fifth century, Augustine championed the biblical emphasis on salvation by grace through faith (Ephesians 2:8-9). He condemned the teachings of *Pelagius, whom Augustine accused of works righteousness in regard to both salvation and *spiritual formation. Because God is sovereign, it is hubris (Gk., "pride") on the part of people that they—as humans—contribute anything to the work of God. Lutheran and Reformed traditions have been greatly influenced by Augustinianism. *See also* semi-Augustinianism.

B

baptism. A *ritual of initiation into Christianity that involves water. In *Scripture, baptism occurs as a faithful act of obedience, and it serves to incorporate people into the *church. Some Christians consider baptism a *sacrament, which serves as a means of saving grace; other Christians consider baptism to be more of an ordinance, which serves as a symbol of *salvation. Jesus served as the model for participation in baptism, and baptism was repeatedly commanded of those who become part of the church. Sacramental views of baptism emphasize the spiritual empowerment mediated by participation in it. Ordinance-oriented views of baptism emphasize the unmerited favor of God's *grace, and the ongoing spiritual empowerment available through the Holy *Spirit.

baptism, believer's. The affirmation that only believers, who have reached an age of accountability (or *reason) and made a profession of *faith, should be baptized. Advocates for believer's baptism argue that people experience the greatest spiritual benefit through their conscious *conversion and instruction in the meaning of baptism.

baptism, infant (or paedobaptism). The affirmation and practice that infants should be baptized, based on the *faith and authority of *churches to administer *sacraments. Advocates for infant baptism argue that people experience the greatest spiritual benefit through the faithful decision by parents and the church, emphasizing that *salvation is a gift, given by God's *grace. There are biblical examples of entire households being baptized, presumably including children (e.g., Acts 2:38-39; 16:15). In both the Catholic and Orthodox traditions, biblical instruction is later given to those who are baptized as infants, so that they may grow in faith and confirm their salvation when they reach an age of accountability (or reason). In Catholic traditions, the sacrament of *confirmation is received when baptized children reach this age and affirm their faith. In the Orthodox tradition, infants are baptized and then immediately *chrismated (anointed with *oil as a seal of the gift of the Holy *Spirit). Chrismation is a sacrament in Orthodox churches. Infant baptism is also practiced by some Protestants—for example, in the Lutheran, Reformed, and Anglican traditions.

baptism with the Holy Spirit. That which John the Baptist promised would go together with the ministry of *Jesus Christ (e.g., Matthew 3:11). It occurred, at least, at the time of *Pentecost in fulfillment of Joel 2:28-32 (see Acts 2:16-21). Traditionally, baptism with the Holy Spirit has been thought to occur at the time of conversion. However, *Pentecostals believe that it occurs subsequent to conversion, as a distinct experience of divine *grace. Classic Pentecostalism believes that speaking in *tongues is the initial evidence of baptism with the Holy Spirit and is followed by other *gifts of the Holy Spirit, which empower Christians for *spiritual formation and ministry. Some Pentecostals distinguish between baptism "by" the Holy Spirit, referring to conversion, and baptism "with" (or "in") the Holy Spirit, referring to the empowerment and spiritual fullness available to Christians.

basic prayer. Formulaic prayers commonly prayed by Christians. Basic Catholic prayers, for example, include the *Our Father (*Lord's Prayer), *Hail Mary, Apostles' Creed, *Glory Be, and prayerful *petitions to *saints and guardian *angels.

beatific vision. The experience of immediate presence and *union (or communion) with God. In medieval Christianity, the beatific vision generally referred to a final reward, where after death a Christian sees God face-to-face (e.g., 1 Corinthians 13:12). This experience of the beatific vision is thought to be accompanied by the fullest experience of human *joy.

beatitude, beatitudes. A literary form expressing great blessedness. In beatitudes, blessings are pronounced over people (or groups of people) on the basis of an action or state of being. Beatitudes are found in both the OT (e.g., Psalm 106:3) and the

NT (e.g., Matthew 5:3-11). The most famous beatitudes are those found at the beginning of the Sermon on the Mount. Beatitudes encourage faithful living through the promise of *blessing.

bedtime prayer. Prayer before going to sleep, often done by parents with children. Topics tend to include thanks for the day past, concerns for others or oneself, and trust that God will look after things while one sleeps.

belief. An affirmation about God and matters related to God, including people's biblical and theological affirmations. Spiritually, people's belief (or *faith) pertain to the particular beliefs, values, and practices that undergird their Christian life and *spiritual formation.

Benedictine spirituality. The *monastic spirituality inspired by Benedict of Nursia, which follows the *Rules of Benedict for community life and *spiritual formation. In the sixth century, Benedict wrote guidelines for monastic living, which helped establish independent monasteries, with ordered living and spiritual guidance, without being overly ascetic. Individuals in Benedictine monasteries vowed to remain within the community and to obey the community's superior (abbot, vicar), for the sake of *praying and working (Lat., *ora et labora*, "pray and work"). A long-term practice of Benedictine spirituality is *lectio divina.

benediction. A closing spoken *prayer for divine assistance or parting exhortation, usually in public *worship. Benedictions were notably included in biblical writings (e.g., Numbers 6:23-27; Ephesians 6:23). The pronouncement of a benediction is a long-standing church tradition, emphasizing the importance of prayer, in particular, prayers of *blessing and *intercession.

Bible. *See* Scripture.

biographies, spiritual. *Stories about the spiritual lives of people that inspire spirituality in others. Such stories may be biographical or autobiographical. Some find spiritual autobiography helpful in gaining greater insight into their *spiritual formation.

black spirituality. A spirituality distinctive of some black Christians. Although many types of spirituality exist, African American Christians and churches emphasize certain characteristics of their collective spirituality. For example, characteristics of black spirituality may include beliefs, values, and practices reflective of African heritage. The impact of centuries of slavery and ongoing racism in the United States have also influenced liberative expressions of black spirituality (*see* liberation). Other characteristics include gospel *music, *singing, and other *worship practices distinctive of African Americans (e.g., spirituals, blues). Black spirituality has heightened contemporary awareness of the *contextual nature of spirituality and the importance of being responsive to the influence of race, ethnicity, and culture on Christian living and *spiritual formation. Exemplars of black spirituality in the United States include Sojourner Truth in the nineteenth century and Martin Luther King Jr. in the twentieth.

blessing. A spiritual and physical benefit given by God. In *Scripture, God blesses all of creation, as well as individuals and groups of individuals (e.g., Israel). There are conditions for receiving God's blessings, and disobedience toward God results in the removal of blessings, and possible curses. Those who bless God express their *praise and *thanksgiving (e.g., Nehemiah 9:5), and people may bless others in the name of God (e.g., Numbers 6:24-26). Public blessings may be spoken or read in church services, for example, in a *benediction. Spiritually, stating blessings for others is a common way of *praying for their spiritual and physical well-being.

bondage. The state of being bound, physically or spiritually, to a power or behavior, which cannot be escaped. In *Scripture, God liberates Israelites from the bondage of slavery. Spiritually, people may experience bondage to sin and death, demonic bondage, or bondage to addictive behaviors or habits. *Jesus Christ worked to set free, physically and spiritually, those who are in bondage (e.g., Luke 4:18). *See also* liberation.

Book of Common Prayer. A prayer book created by Thomas Cranmer and the Church of England in the sixteenth century that contains numerous aids for *worship, including the *liturgy (or structured order) of public *worship services, daily prayers (e.g., Morning Prayer, Evening Prayer; *see* Hours), wording for occasional services (e.g., *baptism, *marriage), and other scriptural and liturgical readings. The Book of Common

Prayer has been edited and revised many times, and in some churches has been replaced, for example, by the book titled *Common Worship*. But many Christians, both inside and outside of Anglicanism, continue to use the Book of Common Prayer as a guide for their personal *spiritual formation as well as for public worship.

bread. Religiously, unleavened bread was important for Judaism because of its use in celebrating Passover. With regard to *salvation, *Jesus Christ called himself the "bread of life" (John 6:35). Bread became ritualistically important for Christians when Jesus blessed and served bread to his disciples during their last supper together. Bread then became sacramentally important, along with *wine, in partaking of the *Eucharist (or *Lord's Supper, *Communion). The use of bread in the Eucharist represents Jesus' physical death and resurrection in order that people may be saved by *grace through *faith. The Catholic and Orthodox churches believe that the bread of the Eucharist becomes the actual body of Jesus through the calling down of the Holy *Spirit through the prayers of the priest. Protestants often talk about bread as a sign of Jesus' body.

breath prayer. Repetition of breathy prayers, either of one's own creation, from *Scripture, or from the *liturgy, in order to clear the mind of other thoughts and replace it with thoughts about God. The breath prayer may be inaccurately named; if prayer is talking to or with God, then breath prayer is, strictly speaking, not conversation but *meditation, with the exception of petitionary forms of the breath prayer. For instance, the *Jesus Prayer is an ancient form of breath prayer, and it is a *petition: "Lord Jesus Christ, Son of God, have mercy on me, a sinner."

C

calendar, Christian (Christian Year, Church Year, or Liturgical Year). An annual calendar of seasons based on key events of the life, death, and resurrection of *Jesus Christ. These seasons include *Advent (and Christmas), Epiphany, *Lent, *Easter, and Ordinary Time (though certain names vary by tradition). Also included are major church events, *holy days, and the celebration of *saints. Participation in this calendar is intended to enrich the lives of believers through creating opportunity for remembrance and through leading believers through spiritual practices, such as mourning, *fasting, and celebration, on an annual cycle. The seasons also enhance expectation and anticipation of the major church events, celebrating all that Jesus has done for our *salvation and *spiritual formation. The rhythm of the Christian year helps believers maintain their own spiritual rhythm, which aids their spiritual development and ministry to others.

calling. A strong sense of divine leading. It may involve an individual call to *salvation; it may also involve a call to ministerial *service (e.g., Ephesians 4:1, 4). Callings to ministerial service may occur individually, or they may occur in response to a corporate or church calling. Although a call or calling is most often associated with ordained ministry, Christians may experience a divine call to lay ministries or to secular *vocations.

calling, effectual. The affirmation that God's call to individuals for their *salvation is irresistible. Reformed theology considers God's election of people to be decreed by God, unconditionally predetermined (e.g., John Calvin). The *grace of God works effectually for people's salvation and for their spiritual development.

candles, prayer (or votive candles). Candles lit in offering a *prayer, wish, or desire to God. Sometimes called votive candles, they suggest the making or fulfillment of a vow made to God. In Orthodox churches, candles represent a prayer, and the flame of the candle signifies the light of *Jesus Christ.

canticle. A song, generally a *hymn or *psalm, taken from biblical texts outside the book of Psalms (e.g., *Magnificat, Song of Zechariah). Typically, these songs are used liturgically as part of the daily *Hours and focus on praising God.

Carmelite spirituality. A *monastic spirituality shaped by an eleventh-century religious order of the Roman Catholic Church, whose members became well-known proponents of *contemplative and mystical spirituality. In the sixteenth century, Teresa of Ávila founded the Discalced Carmelites (or Barefoot Carmelites), which was a mendicant offshoot of the Carmelite order in Spain. Teresa emphasized the ascent of the *soul to God through four stages of *prayer: mental prayer (or contemplative prayer), quiet prayer, devotion of union, and devotion of ecstasy. Teresa was joined in Spain by John of the Cross, who is prominent for his description of mystical ascent after needed *purification, known as the *dark night of the soul.

catechism. A summary of *Scripture and Christian teachings that provides an outline of Christian beliefs, values, and practices. Sometimes called an outline of the faith, catechisms are used by both Catholic and confessional Protestant churches for teaching foundational doctrines to new believers and children (*see* confirmation) before becoming full members of a *church. Catechisms may be used to inspire *spiritual formation as well for instruction in basic Christianity.

celebration. The expression of joy and happiness, especially over God's blessings. In *Scripture, the apostle Paul talks about celebrating the sacrifice of *Jesus Christ for *salvation (1 Corinthians 5:7-8). Celebration usually occurs outwardly and publicly, but it may also occur in subdued ways. In a Christian context, celebration is considered a *spiritual discipline that enables deeper Christian devotion and a fuller experience of life.

celibacy. A spiritual discipline of abstinence from sexual relations. Roman Catholic clergy, *monks, and nuns take a vow of celibacy in support of their *calling, as have others in church history. Orthodox deacons and priests may marry before *ordination; bishops and monastics are celibate. The apostle Paul encouraged people to remain celibate for the sake of ministry, and also to abstain from sexual relations for a set amount of time in order to devote themselves in *prayer to God (see 1 Corinthians 7:1-9).

centering prayer. The act of clearing one's mind by focusing on a sacred phrase, word, or symbol, in order to become aware of God's indwelling presence. Like *breath prayer, centering prayer is not conversational, but more of a *meditation. Rather than focusing on God as separate from us but with whom we are in relationship, in centering prayer we focus on God as found at the center of our being.

cessationism. The belief that the spiritual *gifts ceased after the first century, and that more complete revelation of God, *salvation, and *spiritual formation is found in *Scripture. Reflective of such verses as 1 Corinthians 13:8, the spiritual gifts of *prophecy and *tongues ceased, along with other giftings such as *apostleship, works of *healings, and other miraculous giftings. Thus spiritual formation should focus more on Scripture and obedience to it. *See also* continuationism.

chalice. The cup that is used to offer Holy *Communion, and as such is revered. In Orthodox churches, the chalice contains both the consecrated *bread and *wine, while in Catholic churches it contains the consecrated wine only; the bread is distributed separately.

chant. A rhythmic, melodic recitation of *Scripture, *psalms, *liturgy, and other spiritual *songs. Chanting appears to have been important for *worship in the OT, and chanting became a prominent art form as well as worship practice in medieval Christianity. Chanting continues to be prominent among *high church worship services in *prayer to God and for spiritual edification. In Orthodox churches, the Divine Liturgy as well as most other services are chanted as a continuous *hymn of *praise to God.

charism. A special enabling or spiritual focus given by the Holy *Spirit. Charisms (Gk., *charismata*, "graces") refer to the many ways by which believers minister to the spiritual and material needs of others; some Christians view them as supernaturally given enablements, known as *gifts of the Spirit. The latter translate *charismata* as "spiritual gifts" rather than charisms, but spiritual gifts have a more specific meaning and are usually limited in number.

charismatic movement. A renewal movement of *Pentecostal spirituality during the mid-twentieth century that renewed existing churches, both Catholic and Protestant. Historically, the Pentecostal and charismatic movements are distinguished from one another, but they have similar beliefs, values, and practices, especially with regard to *baptism with the Holy Spirit and the spiritual *gifts.

chrismation. A sacrament in Orthodox churches by which a baptized person receives the gift of the Holy *Spirit through being anointed with the *oil of myrrh.

Christ, Jesus. *See* Jesus Christ.

Christ-centered prayer (or Christocentric prayer). Prayer focused especially on the person of *Jesus Christ, our Savior and Lord, often praying in the name of Jesus. Christ-centered prayer does not negate prayer to other persons of the *Trinity—Father and Holy *Spirit. Instead, it emphasizes the person and work of Jesus for our salvation, as a role model for how people are to live their lives as Christians, and for their *spiritual formation. Christ-centered prayers, for example, the "soul of Christ" (*anima Christi*), are used in *Ignatian spiritual exercises.

Christian. One who professes Christianity, who is a follower of *Jesus Christ. The term is derived from the Greek word *christos* (Christ). The followers of Jesus were first called Christians (*christianoi*) in Antioch (Acts 11:26). Spiritually, Christians are those who seek to *imitate Christ in their lives, as well as follow his teachings as found in *Scripture.

Christian year. *See* calendar, Christian.

Christlikeness. A way Christians describe the quality of spiritual life God has called them to manifest as believers and followers of Jesus Christ. For example, Ephesians 5:1-2 says: "Therefore be imitators of God, as beloved children, and live in love, as Christ loved us." Christlikeness is another way of talking about Christian spirituality, *holiness, *godliness, *maturity, or *perfection.

Christmas. The annual celebration of the birth of *Jesus Christ. It is one of the most sacred festivals of the Christian calendar and immediately follows *Advent. Christmas celebrates the advent (or coming) of the savior Jesus. This *holy day continues to inspire people for their *salvation as well as for their spiritual strengthening through Christmas *worship services, *teachings, *songs, and *traditions of giving that reflect God's gift of Jesus.

Christology. The doctrine of *Jesus Christ, who he is and what he has done and is doing, including his life and *teachings. Jesus not only lived, died, and was resurrected for the *salvation of humankind, but also provided a model for the fullness of human life (e.g., 1 Peter 2:21; 1 John 2:6). Those who are saved are exhorted to live *Christlike lives, and thus the study of Jesus becomes especially important for *spiritual formation. In both

*Scripture and church history, Christians have emphasized *imitating Jesus as a model for their lives, spiritually and in other ways. Although how Jesus was God incarnate—being both fully divine and fully human—is a *mystery, Christians are to follow him for living a godly life and for their spiritual formation.

church. The assembly or community of believers in *Jesus Christ. In *Scripture, the church is described as a local assembly (Gk., *ekklēsia*) of believers, or as the church universal. Early church services were composed of common *prayer, *worship, apostolic *teachings, and other *rites and *rituals. Spiritually, the church has been integral to the teaching and discipling of Christians. Jesus promises to build the church (Matthew 16:18-19), and church members are to proclaim the *gospel, do what is good and just, and grow in Christian *maturity—as individuals and collectively. Churches help people grow in Christ (Ephesians 4:15), in understanding (Hebrews 6:1), and in character (2 Corinthians 9:10). Christians are to pray for the church, as they are to pray for themselves, and for how the church may bless them. The Nicene Creed describes the church as one, holy, catholic (i.e., universal), and apostolic. Later Protestants believed that churches should focus on the proclamation of Scripture and the due administration of sacraments. Catholics and Protestants disagree with regard to both the nature of apostolic authority and due administration of the *sacraments. All Christians emphasize the importance of gathering together in churches for the sake of worship and *fellowship, and for ministering to others.

church walk (or cross walk). A church event, usually on Good Friday, when the congregation of a church takes turns carrying a *cross. Normally this is an opportunity to meditate on the *passion of *Jesus Christ. Along with the church walk, some Christians around the world perform a realistic reenactment of the passion narrative of *Scripture as a spiritual exercise.

Church year. *See* calendar, Christian.

collect. A short liturgical *prayer used to gather together people's worshipful focus at the beginning of a religious assembly or church service. It may also serve as a prayer that combines together the prayers of many who have come to pray and *worship. A simple collect may include a short prayer of *petition, focusing on a single topic, such as grace or forgiveness. Formal collects may include several components: invocation, *praise, petition, aspiration, pleading, and doxology.

commissioning prayer. A *prayer for when a church is setting someone or something aside for a specific task. For example, the early church commissioned Paul and Barnabas for ministry with *fasting, prayer, and the laying on of *hands (Acts 13:2-3). Commissioning prayers may be for pastors, missionaries, ministries, or buildings.

Communion (Holy Communion). One of the names for the *sacrament celebrating *Jesus Christ's last supper with his disciples, which derives from *communio* (Lat., "sharing in common"; cf. Gk. *koinōnia*) and is one of the most common descriptions of the sacrament used by Christians. *See also* Eucharist; Lord's Supper.

communion of saints. A phrase from the Apostles' Creed referring either to the general concept of spiritual union among Christians or specifically to the spiritual union of Christians in the act of liturgical worship. Protestants, Catholics, and Orthodox tend to differ, however, on their view of the communion of the saints. For example, with regard to *intercession, Roman Catholics and Orthodox believe in the invocation of *saints— departed Christians, who are "with the Lord" (2 Corinthians 5:8) and who intercede in prayer on behalf of those who are still alive—and Protestants do not. However, many Protestant *traditions believe that we *worship God along with the communion of saints, including those both alive and deceased.

compassion. *Love manifest in ways that empathize with and sometimes enter into the *suffering of others, especially through tangible expressions of aid for them. Compassion literally means to "suffer with." It is an expression of love that ministers physically as well as spiritually.

Compline. The final evening office of the Hours. Compline varies among Catholic, Orthodox, and Protestant traditions, ranging from an evening service or *Mass, where the congregation publicly recites a number of *psalms and sings *hymns, to private evening prayers, often read after dinner. (The Greek and

Slavonic words for Compline literally mean "after supper.") Compline tends to focus on *contemplation and spiritual peace, especially within *monastic traditions, but may also include *confession and *penitence. In the Orthodox tradition, if more than one person is praying, then mutual forgiveness is usually asked at the end of Compline.

concert of prayer. Group prayers wherein Christians—inside or outside church services—are guided through various *spiritual exercises or themes. A concert of prayer is often accompanied by worship music and *singing.

conference, Christian. A gathering of Christians for religious or ecclesiastical purposes. Although Christian conferences may be used to describe any Christian gathering, they usually refer to extrachurch gatherings intended for spiritual purposes. Christian conferences include midweek services and prayer meetings, small group meetings and Bible studies held in churches or homes, and small groups of Christians who hold one another accountable for *spiritual formation and ministry to others. John Wesley developed an elaborate network of Christian conference meetings, designed for building up Christians and for *service to others, which supplemented Sunday worship services.

confession (of belief). The pronouncement of one's basic beliefs, including one's religious values and practices. Individuals may confess their beliefs, and churches may do so collectively. Formal confessions include *creeds, ecclesiastical confessions, and ecumenical covenants that become standards of doctrine and ministry. Confessional pronouncements are considered spiritually edifying as well as ministerially beneficial.

confession (of sin). The admission of *sin and guilt to God or others. God requires confession for the forgiveness of sins (e.g., 1 John 1:8-10). Confession may be expressed in prayer to God and may involve confession to others (e.g., James 5:16). Confession can be individual or corporate, and it contributes to spiritual *healing. The Catholic sacrament of reconciliation used to be known as the sacrament of confession, and still is in Orthodox churches. In the Catholic tradition acts of *penance may be prescribed, such as the saying of *prayers or acts of reparation when injustice has been done. Confession is important for one's salvation, for one's healing from the effects of sin, for restoring *justice, and for growing in God's *grace. In Orthodox churches, confession is essential for spiritual healing and is an integral part of preparing to receive Holy *Communion. It takes place in the church with no barrier between priest and penitent, who faces the *icon of Jesus Christ, while confessing and receiving *absolution, along with counsel and penance if needed.

confessional. A designated small enclosure in Catholic churches where one may privately and anonymously confess to a priest who sits behind a curtain or screen. The priest may provide counsel, prescribe acts of *penance, and extend *absolution to those who confess their sins.

confidentiality. Holding in confidence information told by others, individually or collectively, when privacy is needed. Confidentiality is essential for the accountability required in holding one another responsible for *spiritual formation. It resembles the *spiritual discipline sometimes known as secrecy, which holds in trust the secrets or sensitive information of others.

confirmation. Spiritual training for converts and youth who have reached the age of accountability (or *reason). Some churches require the completion of confirmation before partaking of the sacrament of *Eucharist. Catholic churches consider confirmation a *sacrament, when those who were baptized as infants may confirm their faith. In Orthodox churches, confirmation is called *chrismation because of the holy *oil (chrism) used, and it takes place either immediately after *baptism or when a previously baptized person receives the Orthodox faith.

congregational prayer. Prayer as a part of a church's large group gathering for *worship or for other types of services. Usually an individual prays, though the opportunity may be given to the congregation as a whole to pray. Korean Christians promote *tongsong-kido* (Kor., "unison prayer"), which emphasizes the importance of communal prayer that is vocal, often loud, and passionate.

consecrate. The hallowing of something or someone, especially for the *service of God. In the OT, objects and priests were consecrated for divine use. In the NT, believers are exhorted to consecrate themselves entirely to God, offering themselves as a "living sacrifice," which is their "spiritual worship" (Romans 12:1).

consolation and desolation. Key terms in *Ignatian spirituality having to do with *self-examination and *discerning the spiritual quality of one's experiences during the day. Self-examination of positive (consolations) and negative (desolations) occurrences helps Christians to assess their spiritual well-being and determine appropriate responses to future challenges in life.

constant prayer. An attitude based on the exhortation to "pray without ceasing" (1 Thessalonians 5:17), which refers more to an ongoing attitude of prayerfulness than literal consecutive prayer. Christians have always emphasized the importance of constancy in prayer.

contemplation. Deep spiritual reflection or thought on God. It may be individual or collective, directed or undirected, conscious or subconscious. Although *Scripture does not frequently mention contemplation (e.g., Isaiah 52:15), it became important to Christians in the early church to talk about the depth of reflection and relationship that one may have with God. *Mystics consider contemplation one of the most important means by which believers experience *union or communion with God. One may contemplate Scripture; for example, Gospel contemplation involves reading a narrative story, usually from the Gospels, and then imagining the details that fill in the scene and engaging God in the story. However, in Christian mysticism, contemplation represents the culmination of several stages. These stages begin with the purgation (*see* purification) from attachments to the world (including *sin), meditation on God that brings spiritual *illumination, and culminating in the immediate contemplation, communion, and union with God.

contemplative spirituality. A type of spirituality that emphasizes *contemplation, often in conjunction with other *spiritual disciplines. Spirituality matures as God works in the lives of believers as they participate in the various disciplines described in *Scripture. Spiritual growth is thought to occur gradually as God works graciously with people for their *purification and *sanctification. In *mystical traditions of Christianity, contemplation is considered the height of spirituality, being the final of three stages: purification (purgative way), *meditation (illuminative way), and *union with God (*unitive way).

contextuality of spirituality. The recognition that all aspects of human life, including spirituality, are influenced by their particular situation or context. With regard to discerning one's spiritual status, sociocultural aspects (e.g., race, ethnicity, gender, class, religion) of one's background and community are considered. It is also important to think about such aspects when evaluating and implementing spiritual practices in one's life, or in churches. Although it is God who brings the spiritual growth, it is important for people to "plant" and "water" wisely in ways that integrate specific life situations, scriptural teachings, and church traditions (1 Corinthians 3:6).

continuationism. The belief that the spiritual *gifts, as supernatural endowments given by God's *Spirit to Christians, continue today, and are as spiritually important as they were in the first century for the empowerment of believers and for building up the *church. Continuationism also emphasizes the ongoing work of God to perform *miracles and *healings, to empower Christians to speak prophetically, and to carry out other *charisms. *Pentecostal and *charismatic Christians are the best-known examples of continuationism, but other Christians also believe in the ongoing work of the Holy Spirit to empower people and churches, for their *spiritual formation as well as for ministry. *See also* cessationism.

conversational prayer. Prayer that occurs in an intimate, familiar tone. Just as *Jesus Christ referred to his heavenly father as *Abba*, which was a term of filial intimacy, Christians find it helpful to address God in prayer conversationally, emphasizing a similar familial intimacy.

conversion. The process whereby people, by *grace through *faith, become Christians. Although conversion has been variously understood, those in *Scripture who became Christians were known as converts (e.g., 1 Corinthians 16:15). Conversion is often thought to include both a turning to God in faith and a turning from *sin in *repentance. The impact of conversion grows through God's regenerative work of *sanctification. Some

Christians distinguish between those who are once-born and twice-born: once-born people gradually grow in their faith and understanding as Christians; twice-born people experience an event (e.g., season of transition or crisis experience) of transformation in their faith and understanding as Christians.

corporate prayer (or collective prayer, group prayer). Prayer performed in a group setting. Most often corporate prayer occurs in public worship services, civic events, gatherings of family and friends, or spontaneous times of prayer. It may occur as part of the *liturgy, extemporaneous prayer (*see* prayer, extemporaneous), or individuals praying silently in the presence of others. Also common are voluntary prayer meetings that occur midweek. In the digital age, global prayer meetings are now possible, during which Christians and churches around the world pray together for specific needs.

courage (or fortitude). The virtue of bravery that Christians consider important in following *Jesus Christ and for living a godly life. In the OT, God gives courage to those who, through faithful obedience, face adversity and enemies. In the NT, the early Christians were thought to be courageous in proclaiming the *gospel, despite persecution. God gives courage to those who pray (e.g., Hebrews 4:14-16). Courage is one of the cardinal virtues (*see* virtues, cardinal).

covenant. An agreement between people, or between God and people, often involving spiritual conditions for the agreement. In *Scripture, fidelity to covenantal relationship with God was inextricably bound up with their spiritual well-being. God initiates several covenants in Scripture. The old covenant represents an agreement God made with Moses and Israel, for their *salvation and godly living. Fidelity to this covenant resulted in *blessings for this life and for life hereafter. The new covenant represents the salvation *Jesus Christ has made available to people by *grace through *faith (Luke 22:20). Fidelity to this covenant likewise results in blessings for this life and for life hereafter, both for salvation and for godly living.

covenant prayer. A prayer of dedication (or rededication) to covenantal relationship with God. In the seventeenth century, Richard Alleine originated covenant prayers, which influenced later Christians, in offering *devotion and surrender to God's will.

creation-centered spirituality. Spirituality that emphasizes God's creation, which must be valued and cared for, and provides tangible means for spiritual expression and formation. Creation-centered spirituality respects God's command to have "dominion" over the world (Genesis 1:28) as caring for creation, which includes care for the environment as well as people. Creation care, also known as Christian environmentalism, represents an expression of spiritual concern and ministry.

creed. A statement that summarizes core Christian beliefs, agreed on by a religious community. The Nicene Creed and Apostles' Creed were among the first statements agreed on by the early church. The creeds were based on previous "rules of faith" (Lat., *regula fidei*), which were ancient summarizations of Christian beliefs and values. During the first eight centuries, there were seven ecumenical (or universal) councils, which have held varying degrees of authority among Catholic, Orthodox, and Protestant churches. Creeds provide Christians a helpful summary of biblical beliefs and values, and they can be used for catechetical training and for *spiritual formation. The recitation of creeds, ancient and modern, is often used in public and private *worship, instructing people's minds as well as their spirits.

cross. The instrument of death in *Jesus Christ's crucifixion, which has become the most recognized image for identifying Christianity. Originally a symbol of shame, the cross eventually came to symbolize the victory of Jesus Christ's death and resurrection. It also has become a powerful image on which Christians focus for *encouragement, *meditation, and *contemplation.

cross, sign of the (or crossing oneself). A *blessing invoked through tracing with one's hand the shape of a cross, either on or hovering above one's body, while praying the *trinitarian formula, silently or audibly. The gesture and *prayer have different meanings in particular church traditions. In addition, there are variations in the how the sign of the cross is made by Catholic, Orthodox, and Protestant Christians. Typically, Orthodox Christians cross from right to left using three fingers (index, middle, and thumb) to represent the *Trinity, while Western traditions cross from left to right, using a varied number of fingers. The sign of the cross is an ancient prayer of the Christian *church.

crucified with Christ. A phrase found in Galatians 2:19, representing a convert's identification with *Jesus Christ in his death. Converts no longer live according to the *law, being guilty of *sin and death, but by *faith they have new life because Jesus now lives within them (Galatians 2:20). The old life is understood as a life captive to the influence of sin. Only through being spiritually crucified and *resurrected with Jesus can believers have new life.

crying prayer. Crying that occurs instead of or together with formal prayer. These tears of joy or sorrow are simply prayer in which the body is allowed to respond holistically (both vocally and emotionally). Crying prayer reminds us of the intensity people may experience emotionally as well as spiritually when they pray. Some Christians call it the gift of tears.

D

dance, liturgical. Artistic human movement employed as a form of *worship. Liturgical dance is considered helpful for promoting spirituality and worship. In *Scripture, people danced as expressions of joy and praise to God (e.g., Exodus 15:20; 2 Samuel 6:14; Psalm 150:4). In church services, believers may participate in liturgical dance to enhance spiritual worship of congregants.

dancing prayer. A type of prayer in which the whole body becomes the means for communication with God. Dancing prayers are sometimes integrated into church *liturgies. They may be as simple as a procession or as intricate as choreographed dances, in which the dancer is communicating to God on behalf of the church (*see* intercession). Dancing prayer is uncommon in churches, though it can be an effective way for individuals to involve the entire self—the whole body, along with emotion and voice—in the act of prayer.

dark night of the soul. A description of the spiritual desperation, purgation, and searching one experiences before turning to God. In the sixteenth century, the Carmelite John of the Cross coined the phrase "dark night of the soul" as an essential stage in *contemplative spirituality. The imagery of a dark night has resonated with people for centuries: first, in *purifying people's senses and spirits, and second, in aiding them in pursuit of *union and communion with God. The dark night of the soul describes the difficulty of becoming detached from the encumbrances of this life in order have a mystical encounter with God.

day of obligation, holy. Certain Roman Catholic *holy days on which church members are expected to attend worship services, such as *Mass. *Sundays, *Christmas, and *Easter are holy days of obligation.

day of prayer. A day set aside for the sake of prayer. Typically days of prayer are set aside for public prayers by a nation, state, or community, and may be ecumenical and interfaith in orientation.

dedication. An initial act of devoting someone or something to God. Dedicating oneself involves making a choice to follow God, and making significant life changes to follow through on that choice. In nonsacramental church traditions, parents may dedicate their infant children rather than baptize them. Prayers of dedication are also offered on behalf of something new, for example, a new ministry or home, including prayers for *blessing and protection.

deification. *See* theosis.

demon. A created spiritual being, considered by some to be a fallen *angel, who inhabits the created order and works to thwart God's will and turn people away from God. *Satan leads demons. God allows them power to persuade, *tempt, oppress, possess, and do violence toward people, while they are free at this time to roam the world. *Jesus Christ had power over demons and gave his disciples this power (Matthew 10:8). In Jesus' name, they cast out and thwarted demons (Mark 16:17). Christians engage in varying degrees of engagement with the demonic, sometimes described as *spiritual warfare, for the sake of their spiritual well-being as well as for ministry.

desert elders/fathers. Monastics of the third to fifth centuries who founded desert *monasticism. Individual Christians known as anchorites (from Gk., *anachōrētēs*, "to withdraw") withdrew from the world to deserts, refining *contemplative practices. Monastic communities later were founded around these desert elders, the most famous of whom was Antony the Great in Egypt. The *Apophthegmata*, or *Apophthegmata patrum* (Lat., "sayings of the fathers"), refers to a collection of stories and wisdom sayings from the early monastic period that provide insight into the contemplative lifestyle and *teachings of the desert fathers and mothers.

desolation. *See* consolation and desolation.

detachment, spiritual. The state of being spiritually and, in other ways, unattached and unperturbed from this-worldly interruptions that divert spiritual focus. Detachment corresponds to the kind of spiritual abandonment (*see* abandonment, spiritual) from self-interest, which culminates in disinterested love (*see* love, disinterested) for God.

***Devotio Moderna* (modern devotion).** A religious renewal movement beginning in the fourteenth century that emphasized piety by participating in *spiritual disciplines such as *humility, *obedience, and *simplicity. The *Devotio Moderna* movement also emphasized the need for providing spiritual guidance for laypeople as well as clergy. Geert Groote and Thomas á Kempis are well-known representatives of the *Devotio Moderna*, especially through their emphasis on the *imitation of *Jesus Christ.

devotion. Wholehearted commitment to a person or purpose. *Scripture encourages devotion to God, and Christians are to be devoted to *Jesus Christ (e.g., 1 Corinthians 7:35). Scripture also warns against devoting ourselves to that which is contrary to God (e.g., 2 Corinthians 11:3).

devotional. A short reading, sermon, or talk for the sake of directing devotion to God. Individually, Christians read passages of *Scripture or a collection of inspirational writings to aid their understanding and *love for God. Collectively, brief sermons may be spoken as a kind of devotional for the sake of public worship.

devotions. Personal spiritual practices, prescribed or spontaneous, that provide ways to pray, *study (especially *Scripture), and dedicate oneself to God. Various *spiritual exercises or disciplines may be used for devotional purposes to deepen ones knowledge of and relationship with God. Common Catholic devotions include the *rosary, *stations of the cross, and veneration of the *saints. Devotions may include group teachings or practices intended to help people collectively in their relationship with God. Orthodox Christians often pray the *Jesus Prayer throughout the day, sometimes using a prayer rope or bracelet, as a way of focusing on God.

discernment. Determination of God's presence and role in the events of life. In *Scripture, discernment required that Christians "test the spirits," whether they came from God, false prophets, or a demonic source (1 John 4:1). Spiritually, discernment has been important for self-assessment, for example, in the daily *examen, which is an *Ignatian spiritual exercise. Sometimes people undertake a time of discernment when making important decisions (e.g., *vocation).

discernment, gift of. A special enabling of the Holy *Spirit that empowers believers to determine God's presence and role in the events of life, vis-à-vis false prophets or *demons.

disciple. A personal follower, especially one who follows Jesus Christ. In the NT, Jesus chose twelve disciples (Matthew 10:1-2). But all who follow Jesus are known as disciples. Characteristics of disciples include trusting and loving Jesus, learning from and imitating him, and confessing Jesus to others. Being a disciple requires disciplining oneself to be like the one who is followed and to make others disciples.

discipline of the secret (Lat., *disciplina arcani*). Beliefs and practices kept confidential, due to *mystery surrounding their spiritual nature. In the ancient church, Christians used caution in what they spoke about publicly, due to misunderstandings that arose and to distortions attributed to them. For example, the *Eucharist was misrepresented as cannibalism. Thus care was taken in instructing new converts so that they might rightly understand and practice the *teachings of *Scripture, both for their doctrinal and *spiritual formation.

disciplines, spiritual. *See* spiritual disciplines.

divine appointment. Interactions with another person or persons that are believed to have been arranged by God. They are thought to occur for spiritual purposes, perhaps to comfort, encourage, or guide others.

Divine Liturgy. The primary worship service in Orthodox churches. It is celebrated once each *Sunday by the entire community of worshipers (i.e., parish), offering themselves to God. The Divine Liturgy is a eucharistic service and is focused on the resurrection of Jesus.

dying, art of. Advice on how Christians may deal well with impending death. Latin texts on the art of dying (*ars moriendi*) arose during the fifteenth century in response to the horrors of the black death. In the seventeenth century, Jeremy Taylor wrote *The Rules and Exercises of Holy Dying.* They provide instructions, consolations, and prayers for the dying individual as well as the family and friends of the dying individual.

E

Easter. A Christian *holy day celebrating the resurrection of *Jesus Christ. Often considered the greatest of the Christian *feasts, Easter is marked by numerous *celebrations, *rites, and *rituals. In the Christian *calendar, Easter is preceded by a time of *fasting, *penitence, and *prayer known as *Lent. It is followed by the Easter season (or Eastertide), an extended time of celebration. For Catholics, Easter is a holy *day of obligation. Spiritually, Easter promotes reflection on the significance of Jesus' resurrection and on his procurement of our *salvation, and on the new birth and spiritual growth that converts experience. In Orthodox churches, Easter is usually called Pascha (Gk., Passover) and is considered the "Feast of Feasts," the most important *feast day of the year. As in ancient churches, the Saturday before Pascha (Holy Saturday) is the traditional time for *baptism of catechumens.

ecstasy. A heightened state of *joy resulting from intimacy with God. Sometimes thought of as an out-of-body experience, ecstasy transcends mere communion with God, usually described as union with God. In *Scripture, some consider the apostle Paul's reference to a man "caught up to the third heaven—whether in the body or out of the body I do not know"—as an ecstatic experience (2 Corinthians 12:2).

ecumenism. An emphasis on Christian unity and cooperation in ministry among different churches and denominations, reflective of Jesus' prayer that his disciples be unified (John 17:21). Some Christians consider ecumenism to be an essential expression of their spirituality. Examples of ecumenical spirituality include Philip Schaff (nineteenth century), the rise of various ecumenical organizations in the United States during the twentieth century, including the National Council of Churches and the National Association of Evangelicals, and, worldwide, the World Council of Churches and the World Evangelical Alliance.

edification. The building up or improvement of people for their spiritual well-being. In Christianity, edification is for the holistic maturation of people, which occurs through various means, either by the direct work of God or by one another. People are edified by the *Scriptures and by the presence and work of the Holy *Spirit. Members of the church are to edify one another spiritually through various means, including *prayer and love for one another (e.g., Romans 14:19; 1 Corinthians 12:7-11).

encouragement. The act of giving support and confidence for people's spiritual well-being. Encouragement is a means for edifying others by strengthening their morale, for example, through verbally praising them. In *Scripture, encouragement is sometimes referred to as *exhortation, though some draw a distinction between the two, and is listed as one of the *gifts of the Spirit (Romans 12:8).

enthusiasm. A description of animated expressions of spirituality or *worship of God. Revivalists in the eighteenth century, for example, were called enthusiasts, sometimes due to their spiritual vitality, and other times due to claims of ecstatic visions or revelations. Generally, accusations of enthusiasm were derogatory, though sometimes so-called enthusiasts embraced the term in honor of their spiritual vitality.

eschatology. Doctrine of the end times (Gk., *eschata*, "last things") and their implications for how we live in the present time. Eschatology influences one's view of spirituality, since ideas about the future affect how one lives here and now. Eschatologies that emphasize the imminent return of *Jesus Christ tend to focus more on the need for evangelism, rather than on long-term needs for spiritual and ethical formation. Regardless of one's view of eschatology, Christians are to be as attentive to the spiritual and ethical development of their lives, individually and collectively, as to proclamation of the *gospel.

eternal life. The complete, fulfilled life available to those who are saved by *grace through *faith (e.g., John 3:16). Spiritually, eternal life is significant because, while it extends into eternity, it already has begun.

eternity. Infinite or unending time, which *Scripture uses to describe the timelessness of God vis-à-vis the limitations of finite time experienced by humankind. Christians believe that God can work redemptively and spiritually in the lives of people in all places and at all times because God is not limited by finite time. Because eternity transcends human understanding, Christians wonder whether eternity refers to timelessness (that which exists outside spacetime) or the infinite expanse of time. Regardless, God ministers continuously on behalf of people, for their eternal as well as temporal well-being.

Eucharist. Derived from *eucharistia* (Gk., "thanksgiving"), one of the names for the *sacrament celebrating Jesus Christ's last supper with his disciples. It is particularly used by Catholic, Orthodox, Lutheran, Anglican, and Presbyterian churches. *See also* Lord's Supper; Communion.

evangelical. A term used to describe something related to or focused on the *gospel (Gk., *euangelion*), or "good news" of *salvation through *Jesus Christ. Historically, Martin Luther referred to his theology as evangelical, since one of his goals was to restore emphasis on salvation by *grace through *faith. Contemporary manifestations of evangelical spirituality emphasize the proclamation of the gospel, evangelism, and missions as fulfillment of the *Great Commission (Matthew 28:16-20).

evangelism, gift of. A special enabling of the *Holy Spirit that empowers believers to proclaim the *gospel of *Jesus Christ and *salvation in both word and deed. True evangelism (described as evangelization by Catholics) avoids unscrupulous tactics, sometimes known derogatorily as proselytism.

evil. That which is in opposition to God and God's good will, and is characterized as corruption, depravity, and violence.

Some do not consider evil to be a reality per se, but a priva-
tion of the good, contrary to God's will. *Scripture identifies
evil with *Satan, though it seems to exert power in its own
right. In addition, Scripture warns against evil and doing
evil, and the need for people to wrestle against evil. Scripture
also gives hope for overcoming the curses of evil through the
atonement of *Jesus Christ and for God's ultimate victory over
evil. Reflection on the problem of evil continues to perplex
people, challenging people's spiritual understanding and relationship with God.

examen (or daily examen). A *contemplative time of *prayer with
two primary purposes: becoming conscious of God's presence
and reflecting on the day. The prayer is typically divided into
several phases. First, believers recognize God's presence with
them, reflecting on the positive (consolations) and negative
(desolations) events of the day (*see* consolation and desolation).
Second, believers express gratitude for God's consolations of
the day, and spiritual aid in responding to the desolations.
Third, believers reflect on the day, paying particular attention
to their spiritual interactions with God. Fourth, believers ask
forgiveness if necessary. Last, believers respond in recommit-
ment to God, based on their spiritual reflection. Not all of these
steps need to be followed, nor do they need to be followed se-
quentially. They are intended primarily to help one pray, and
to focus one's consciousness on God. The daily examen often
results in thanksgiving for what God has done and given us, as
well as for spiritual *self-examination and resolve to live more
faithfully. *Ignatius of Loyola in the sixteenth century encouraged practice of the daily examen as a path to understanding
God's presence and work in our lives.

A whimsical contemporary variation of the daily examen is
called Pow, Wow, Holy Cow. This variation encourages people
to share a low point of their day (Pow), a high point of their day
(Wow), and where they saw God in their day (Holy Cow).

exhortation, gift of. A special enabling of the Holy Spirit that
empowers believers to challenge others to obey God or to act
in godly ways. Exhortation is often included among the *gifts
of the Holy *Spirit.

exorcism. The casting out of *demons that either oppress or possess individuals, affecting their spiritual well-being in evil ways. *Jesus cast out demons during his earthly ministry, as did his *disciples (e.g., Matthew 8:16; 10:1). Exorcism is usually thought of as the casting out of demons in those possessed (rather than those oppressed). Some Christians think of exorcism as a *charism, or spiritual *gift.

experience. The sentient dimension of people's lives. Spiritual experience is usually thought of in terms of one's individual encounter with God or others; it may also include corporate experiences of people and God. Often, the experiential dimension of spirituality has to do with the affective, emotional, or passionate aspect of relationship with God and others. Of course, encounters with God might range from ecstatic and peaceful, to fear and trembling. Because the spiritual and physical dimensions of life are inextricably bound up with one another, spiritual experiences ought not ignore physical experiences, and vice versa.

extrasensory perception. An innate ability to perceive spiritual or other realities, possibly including the future, that otherwise are inaccessible to the senses. Some Christians consider such an ability to be beneficial to spirituality, but many do not think that these human abilities—even exceptional ones—contribute to spirituality, which is produced only by God.

F

faith. Assent to and trust in something or someone, based on spiritual perception rather than rational and empirical proof. In *Scripture, faith is the foundational *virtue for *salvation by which God blesses those who believe. Although God intends that Christians grow in faith, their faith may be tested in order to verify it and to help faith grow, by divine *grace. The quality of Christian spirituality is sometimes equated with faith and its formation. It can increase and mature, based on God's ongoing work in the lives of believers, aided by people's voluntary participation in various means of grace (e.g., *spiritual disciplines, *sacraments). *Jesus Christ praised those with great faith, and he admonished those with little faith. People are saved by grace through faith, which is considered a gift from God (Ephesians 2:8). Believers also are encouraged to grow in faith as well as in *hope and *love (*see* virtues, theological). Prayer aids faith development, as do godly attitudes and actions (e.g., Luke 17:5). In medieval Christianity, faith included knowledge (Lat., *notitia*), for example, of the *gospel of Jesus Christ, intellectual assent to that knowledge (Lat., *assensus*), and trust (Lat., *fiducia*)—the entrusting of oneself to God and to the gospel. In Protestant Christianity, emphasis is placed mostly on trust, and on the need to grow in faithful trust of God, both for one's salvation and for growth in Christian *obedience and *spiritual formation.

faith development. Growth in one's faith, which also contributes to growth in one's *hope and *love (*see* virtues, theological). God aids faith development by *grace, as Christians voluntarily obey biblical teachings and practice *spiritual disciplines. Although *Scripture sometimes talks about the presence and absence of faith, it also talks about having "little" faith and "great" faith (e.g., Matthew 8:10, 26; 15:28). This implies that one's faith may grow from little faith to great faith, and Jesus Christ repeatedly exhorted his followers' faith to do so. In church history, Christians have regularly emphasized the importance of developing their faith, realizing that growth in faith is inextricably bound up with growth in hope and love.

faith, gift of. A special enabling of the Holy *Spirit that empowers people to believe in God and God's will (1 Corinthians 12:9). Although all Christians are to have faith, some are believed to have a special gift of it.

familial spirituality. A type of spirituality that emphasizes care for family—grandparents, parents, siblings, spouses, children, and grandchildren. Participation in and care for family is considered a heightened expression of Christian spirituality (e.g., 1 Timothy 5:8). Familial spirituality (or piety) is not always identified with Christianity, but it has a long-standing presence in both *Scripture and church history. Correspondingly, there is a kind of caregiving spirituality wherein Christians provide health care and other needs—physical and spiritual—

for those who cannot care for themselves, and who may not be family members.

fasting. Abstention from food and drink as an act of *devotion, praying and communing with God. Fasting may serve as a *spiritual discipline that enables people to focus on God and Christian formation. *Jesus fasted, though he defended his disciples for not having fasted while he was with them, instead stating that their fasting would be appropriate after his death and resurrection (Matthew 9:14-15). There are many ways to fast, which include different kinds of abstention from food and drink, for short and long periods of time, depending on what is considered conducive to praying and communing with God. Some also abstain from things other than food, such as entertainment and social media, as nondietary forms of fasting. *See also* asceticism.

feast. A group celebration centered on *fellowship and the sharing of food and drink. In *Scripture, feasting is a practice promoting gratitude for God's provisions, community, and creating space for *joy. In liturgical traditions, formal *feast days are celebrated, usually to commemorate a *saint or an event in the life of Jesus or the *church. Modern manifestations of feasting may include potluck meals sponsored by churches.

feast days. Days set aside in the Christian *calendar, for example, by Catholic and Orthodox churches, to commemorate holy events, teachings, and canonized *martyrs and *saints. Jews, as well as some Christian churches, celebrate events that occurred in the OT (e.g., Passover). Feast days are intended to promote remembrance of God's deeds—such as the deliverance of the Jews from Egypt—which encourages faithful obedience. The Christian celebration of feast days also includes key events of *salvation, sometimes known as *holy days (e.g., *Christmas, *Easter), and for the faith and self-*sacrifice of martyrs and saints. Holy days are considered *days of obligation in some church traditions, and members are required to attend worship services in honor of them. Other celebrations are optional, for example, the commemoration of lesser-known martyrs and saints. It is considered a *spiritual discipline to celebrate the *blessings of events related to salvation and to Christian living, and to honor martyrs and saints who serve as role models for those who seek to live godly and service-oriented lives.

fellowship. Friendly association and sharing (Gk., *koinōnia*, "fellowship, sharing"). Early Christians worshiped in the context of fellowship and sharing with one another, considering community and accountability crucial for spiritual growth and ministry (e.g., Acts 2:42). Fellowship encourages hospitality to those outside the church, and unity with those inside it. Throughout church history, Christians and churches have put great emphasis on fellowship and sharing with one another, ecclesiastically and interpersonally. Both for the sake of promoting spiritual growth and for supporting ministry, the biblical concept of *koinōnia* has been a prime focus of *ecumenism. Fellowship is sometimes referred to as a *spiritual discipline having to do with sharing spiritual as well as physical bounty.

feminist spirituality. A spirituality distinctive to women who are concerned about equal standing for themselves before God, as well as before others in *church and society. Since women as well as men have been created in the *image of God, Christians ought to do more to honor their equality (e.g., Genesis 1:27). Characteristics of feminist spirituality include beliefs, values, and practices that encourage an egalitarian relationship between men and women, which are believed to be based on a truer interpretation of Scripture (e.g., Galatians 3:28). Spiritually, feminist spirituality has heightened awareness of the *contextual nature of spirituality and the importance of being responsive to the influence of gender on Christian living and spiritual formation. Forerunners of feminist spirituality include Hildegard of Bingen (twelfth century) and Julian of Norwich (fourteenth century), who conceived of God with both male and female attributes. More contemporary examples from the twentieth century include Katharine Bushnell and Rosemary Radford Ruether. *See also* women's spirituality.

fervent prayer. Prayer in which earnestness and zeal are prominently involved, often associated with outspoken prayer. This type of prayer alludes to James 5:16, in which some translations talk about the effectiveness of fervent prayer. Fervent prayer need not be loud or extemporaneous (*see* prayer, extemporaneous); it can be silent or scripted, as long as it is passionate. Similarly, Jesus encouraged perseverance in prayer, for example, when he "told them a parable about their need to pray always and not to lose heart" (Luke 18:1).

festival. *See* holy days.

fire. In *Scripture the heat and light of combustion can symbolize God's encounter with people. God spoke to Moses from a burning bush (Exodus 3:2-4), and fire appeared on those who received the Holy *Spirit at *Pentecost, attended by speaking in *tongues (Acts 2:3-4). Scripture also speaks of how people's faith is "tested by fire" (like a refiner's fire; see 1 Peter 1:7) when they endure various *trials and tribulations in this life. In church history, fire has repeatedly been used as a symbol for the presence and work of the Holy Spirit, and for the refining of Christians' spiritual lives.

five-finger prayer. Prayer, often following the form of the *Lord's Prayer, in which a person prays a short prayer in each category while holding a finger, then holds the next finger and prays the next part, until all the fingers have been prayed. The prayer is then repeated, returning to the first finger.

flagellation. The self-infliction of physical pain for the sake of *repentance, self-denial, and submission to *spiritual formation. Flagellation may include the whipping or cutting of oneself, which becomes excessive and thwarts the intention of spiritual formation. *See also* asceticism.

flesh, in the. A phrase used to describe earthly matters rather than heavenly matters of the spirit. The apostle Paul warned against living sinfully "in the flesh" or "of the flesh" (Romans 8:3, 8; Galatians 5:19-21). Although the flesh is a part of God's good creation, *Scripture commands that people ought to live lives in the spirit, rather than in the flesh, which leads to worldly, sinful activities.

footwashing. The practice of washing the feet of others as a spiritual act of *service and *humility, which follows the model of *Jesus washing the feet of his disciples (e.g., John 13:1-17). Members of the Anabaptist tradition consider footwashing comparable to a *sacrament, which all should emulate. The act of footwashing can be literal or figurative.

formation, spiritual. *See* spiritual formation.

four-stranded garland, the. A variation of *lectio divina taught by Martin Luther. The four-stranded garland is a metaphor representing different ways one prayerfully approaches *Scripture as instruction, thanksgiving, *confession, and guidance.

free prayer. Prayer offered to strangers or casual acquaintances. Free prayer can be done standing on a corner with a sign that says "free prayer" or by door knocking and offering free prayer. Although the offering of free prayer seems unusual, those who give (and receive) it testify to the power of giving without expectation of receiving.

freedom, human (or free will). Volition, enabled by God's grace, to make choices with regard to people's *salvation and spiritual development. Although salvation is considered a gift of God (Ephesians 2:8), people are expected to respond voluntarily in faith as well as with *repentance and *baptism. Christians differ in how much freedom God gives them, especially considering the adverse effects of *sin on people's choices. But most agree that there occurs both divine gift and human task in people's salvation and spiritual development. Due to sin, human freedom became corrupted, and humans are therefore not capable of meriting salvation or growing spiritually. But by God's *grace, they may be redeemed and mature spiritually. With regard to Christian spirituality, growth comes by God's grace, but people must choose to allow God's *Spirit to work in and through them. Analogous to what Paul says in 1 Corinthians 3:6, we are to "plant" and "water," but it is God who gives the spiritual growth. Correspondingly, as people submit to God by participating in various means of grace described in *Scripture, God aids them in becoming more holy, loving, and Christlike.

friendship. Close relations, partiality, and affection between two or more people. In *Scripture, friends show great love for one another, including care for one another's spiritual well-being. In John 15:13-16, *Jesus called his disciples "friends," emphasizing the intimacy of relationship he has with those who believed in him. Today, friendship serves as an aid to *spiritual formation, as friends support one another spiritually as well as relationally. Historically, friendship has been considered a *virtue, which Christians have also emphasized as a way to deepen one's love for other people, for oneself, and for God.

frugality. A characteristic of simple living, marked especially by thriftiness and material *simplicity. Frugality may serve as a *spiritual discipline that enables people to focus on God and Christian *devotion, rather than being distracted by possessions.

fruit of the Spirit. The *blessings of living by the Spirit, which bears the "fruit" of *love, *joy, *peace, and other godly qualities (Galatians 5:16, 22-23, 25). The apostle Paul contrasts these fruits with "works of the flesh," which prevent one from inheriting the kingdom of God (Galatians 5:19, 21). *Holiness traditions of Christian spirituality especially emphasize the pursuit and development of the fruit of the Spirit.

G

gentleness. The quality of being kind and caring. *Scripture describes gentleness as a result of God's Holy *Spirit at work in the lives of believers, and as such reflects spiritual *maturity (Galatians 5:23). Gentleness is included among the *fruit of the Spirit.

genuflection. Bending one or both knees as a sign of deep respect, especially in spiritual homage to God. In Christianity, genuflection is used within certain church traditions before taking the *Eucharist, and at the *cross. It also is used during various parts of the Catholic and Orthodox *liturgies, especially during *holy days.

geography, spiritual. An image sometimes used by Christians as an analogy to describe their spiritual development. Spirituality is described by earthly ups and downs, with the final goal visualized as a geographical location.

gift of the Holy Spirit. A reference to salvation, when Peter said, "Repent, and be baptized every one of you in the name of Jesus Christ so that your sins will be forgiven; and you will receive the gift of the Holy Spirit" (Acts 2:38). The term may also be used in reference to one of the many gifts of the Holy *Spirit.

gifts of the Holy Spirit. Graces or enablings of the Holy *Spirit that empower believers spiritually beyond their human abilities.

Scripture describes gifts as an outflow of *love, which edifies others. As such, the variety of gifts serve to unify the church, locally and around the world, ministering to people outside as well as inside churches. Throughout church history, the "gifts" (Gk., *charismata*) have been understood in various ways. Catholic, Orthodox, Anglican, and other Christians have described them as "charisms," a transliteration of *charismata*, which refer to the many ways that God empowers believers for spiritual growth and ministry. *Pentecostals believe that spiritual gifts are uniquely given to believers, subsequent to *conversion, when they experience baptism with the Holy Spirit (or *baptism in the Holy Spirit). In classic Pentecostalism, speaking in *tongues is ordinarily thought to be the tangible evidence of Holy Spirit baptism. Gifts may be temporary, given for a specific reason on a specific occasion, or they can be readily available to the believer for future use. Some Pentecostals believe that 1 Corinthians 12:4-11 describes nine spiritual gifts: *prophecy, *healing, working *miracles, tongues, interpretation of tongues (*see* tongues, interpretation of), *wisdom, *knowledge, *faith, and *discernment. But there exist other lists that include *teaching, *serving, *exhortation, *giving, *giving aid, *compassion, *apostleship, *helps, *administration, *evangelism, and *shepherding (e.g., Romans 12:6-8; 1 Corinthians 12:28; Ephesians 4:11). Other Christian qualities have been added to this list: *grace, martyrdom, *exorcism, *intercession, *hospitality, and *celibacy. There is no consensus among Christians with regard to either the quantity or quality of spiritual gifts. Although it is God who is believed to impart spiritual gifts, Christians are nonetheless encouraged to desire them, especially prophecy (1 Corinthians 14:1-4). All are expected to exercise their various giftings for the sake of ministry and service to others, as well as for their own spiritual *edification.

giving, gift of. A special enabling of the Holy *Spirit that empowers believers to give extraordinarily beyond their means, often in financial ways.

giving aid, gift of. A special enabling of the Holy *Spirit that empowers believers to give aid extraordinarily beyond their means, usually in helping others in tangible, material ways.

Glory Be. A trinitarian doxology (prayer of praise), glorifying the "Father, Son, and Holy Spirit." Used in Catholic and Orthodox Church traditions, the Glory Be is prayed during *liturgies, during the *Hours, and also in conjunction with the *rosary. A version of the prayer in English is as follows: "Glory be to the Father, and to the Son, and to the Holy Ghost; as it was in the beginning, is now, and ever shall be: world without end. Amen." *See also* trinitarian formula.

glory, glorification. Honor and renown, usually given to God. *Scripture tells us to give glory to God (1 Corinthians 10:31). The expression "Glory!" also represents an exclamation of *praise. References to glory (and glorification) may also refer to heaven, or a heaven-like experience on earth, but especially to Christians' full reception of *eternal life in heaven.

glōssolalia. *See* tongues, speaking in.

gnosticism. An ancient Hellenistic philosophy that emphasized knowledge (Gk., *gnōsis*) as the highest good, downplaying the physical dimension of life for the sake of one's spiritual well-being. Although Gnostics influenced some early Christians, Christians mostly criticized Gnosticism for its spiritual reductionism. According to *Scripture, our physical and spiritual lives are inextricably bound up with one another, and both need to be valued and developed.

God. The supreme being, who created the world, providentially cares for it, and purposefully directs all of creation with both love and justice. There are many ways that *Scripture describes God's attributes: holy, sovereign, eternal, knowledgeable, present, wise, righteous, just, judge, empathetic, loving, compassionate, forgiving, redemptive, and restorative. In addition, God is spirit, and people relate with God spiritually as well as in other ways—physically, morally, socially, institutionally (e.g., John 4:24). As such, the spiritual well-being of people primarily has to do with their relationship with God. People were created by God to be in relationship with God (e.g., Revelation 21:3). Moreover, people were created to be in relationship with others (e.g., Genesis 2:18). *Love is to be the highest way of relating with God, and of relating with others—loving our neighbors as we love ourselves (e.g., Mark

12:28-31). Spiritually, people grow in relationship with God by *faith, expressed through various *covenants (e.g., old and new covenants), and by *repenting from *sin and other factors that break people's relationship with God. Through *Jesus Christ, God has provided a way by which people may be saved by *grace through faith, which results in reconciliation with God, reestablishing a right (or righteous) relationship with God. Through the Holy *Spirit, God continues to provide ways by which people may grow in their relationship with God, to love God and others, and grow into greater *Christlikeness through various spiritual means of grace (*see* grace, means of), including spiritual practices, *spiritual exercises, and *spiritual disciplines. Thus for Christians the *image of God in them—distorted by sin—may progressively be restored and perfected, until they receive the fullness of God's spiritual *blessings of *eternal life in heaven. In the meantime, Christians are to be attentive to loving God, loving themselves, and loving others in holistic ways, which minister physically as well as spiritually, individually as well as socially, justly as well as lovingly.

godliness. A way Christians describe the quality of spiritual life that they believe God has called them to manifest as believers and followers of God, especially as revealed in *Jesus Christ. *Scripture says that God's "divine power" enables believers' godliness (2 Peter 1:3); in addition, they are to "train" themselves in godliness (1 Timothy 4:7). Godliness is another way of talking about Christian spirituality, *holiness, *Christlikeness, *maturity, or *perfection.

golden rule. The religious principle summarized in Jesus' words: "Do to others as you would have them do to you" (Luke 6:31), "for this is the law and the prophets" (Matthew 7:12). The golden rule is thought to summarize the biblical mandate to love your neighbor as yourself (Mark 12:31). Fulfilling this principle in all one is, thinks, says, and does is considered among the highest triumphs of Christian spirituality. Variations of the golden rule appear in other religions, though it is identified by Christians as the way to fulfill Christlike living.

gospel. A reference to the message or "good news" (Gk., *euangelion*) of *Jesus Christ about *salvation. For Jesus, proclamation of the gospel represented the coming of God's *kingdom, to which people, in response, are to "repent, and believe in the good news" (Mark 1:15). The salvation to which the gospel testifies includes more than *eternal life; it also includes discipleship and willingness to learn from Jesus, obey him, and suffer on behalf of him.

grace. Unmerited favor and empowerment from God. Grace is given by God for *salvation, and also for *spiritual formation (e.g., John 1:16-17; Romans 1:5). However, with divine grace comes the expectation of human response. Some Christians think that God does everything, and people do nothing, spiritually speaking; other Christians think that God both empowers and expects people to partner synergistically with God's grace. Although people are expected spiritually to "plant" and "water," it is God who gives the growth (1 Corinthians 3:6-7).

grace, common. The belief that God acts graciously in the lives of all people, providentially caring for the world and helping people resist their propensity to *sin and do widespread violence against one another. John Calvin contrasted common grace with saving grace, the latter not being commonly available to all people, due to the limited atonement of *Jesus Christ.

grace, effectual. Grace that works entirely due to God's initiation. For example, the atonement of *Jesus Christ was effected solely by God in providing *salvation for people. Some Christians, especially from Reformed traditions (e.g., John Calvin), believe that all of life is determined by God, who is sovereign, and that grace is irresistible, both for salvation and for *spiritual formation. *See also* grace, prevenient.

grace, irresistible. *See* grace, effectual.

grace, justifying (or saving grace). The divine work of God that rectifies people's righteous standing before him. Since only *Jesus Christ's atonement is thought sufficient for people to be justified, saving grace is that which enables *faith in Jesus, through which his atoning work is applied to individuals.

grace, means of. Biblical ways or channels through which God graciously works in the lives of believers, empowering them for Christian living. In church history, means of grace have been distinguished between general (or informal) and specific (or formal, instituted). General means of grace are similar to what also have been called *spiritual disciplines; specific means of grace refer to the *sacraments. Christians spend most of their time participating in the general means of grace, for example, *prayer, *worship, *study, and so on. The sacraments are considered formal means of grace, since they are believed to have been specifically instituted by *Jesus Christ. John Wesley talked about prudential means of grace, that is, practical ways through which God graciously works in the lives of believers, empowering them for Christian living, for example, in structuring small accountability groups.

grace prayer (or saying grace). *See* prayer at mealtime.

grace, prevenient. Grace given by God that enables people to have the freedom to believe in and love God for their *salvation and for Christian living. Because of the effects of *sin, God gives grace, which precedes people's voluntary decision making but does not determine the outcome of their choices. Catholic and Orthodox Christians believe in prevenient (or preventing, preceding) grace along with later Arminian and Wesleyan Christians, in contrast to the Augustinian belief in effectual grace (*see* grace, effectual) held by Martin Luther and John Calvin. Because of prevenient grace, people may choose to accept or reject God's free gift of eternal life. Their election is conditioned on voluntary *faith and *repentance. Likewise, people may choose to grow spiritually, aided by God's grace. *Spiritual formation requires people's choices, which are preveniently initiated, sustained, and completed by God, but not without their choice to participate.

grace, resistible. Grace that is thought to be given by God, along with the God-given freedom to accept or reject it. The freedom given by God for people to choose undergirds their responsibility for *spiritual formation. Although God gives the spiritual growth, people are to be obedient to the teachings of *Scripture and discipline themselves for growing spiritually.

grace, sanctifying. The divine work of God that renews believers in righteous and godly living. The restoration begins with regeneration, which some Christians refer to as initial *sanctification, and is continued through the presence and power of the Holy *Spirit to make believers holy.

Great Commission. The final charge *Jesus Christ gave to his disciples before his ascension, sending them to go and make *disciples, baptize them, and teach them to obey everything commanded by him (Matthew 28:16-20). Fulfillment of the Great Commission is considered by some Christians to be the high point of spirituality, and so they are zealous in evangelism, missions, and church planting, which is thought to be the first step in making disciples of all nations.

grieving. The process of dealing emotionally with a loss or tragedy in one's life. As people recognize the stages of grief they experience, they may open themselves to God's *grace and *healing for their pain and sorrow as well as for growing personally and spiritually.

group prayer. *See* corporate prayer.

H

habit. A routine action that one has developed, which includes good or bad behavior. In *Scripture, some habits are bad (e.g., "neglecting to meet together," Hebrews 10:25), whereas others are good, especially those habits described as being virtuous or spiritually beneficial. In church history, some Christians have talked about holy habits as a way to affirm spiritual disciplines (or related practices) intended for promoting faithful, holy living. *See also* virtue.

hagiography. A spiritualized or, perhaps, idealized history of a person, church, or movement that focuses on positive accomplishments. Although hagiography may help to honor admirable Christians, including those who are spiritual exemplars, it may also result in an unrealistic and thus misleading role model, which may hurt their followers more than help them.

Hail Mary. A request or petition to *Mary the mother of *Jesus Christ, for *intercession, using parts of Luke 1:28. Also known in Latin as the *Ave Maria*, this prayer is named after the initial two words in the prayer, and it is most commonly practiced by Catholics. Along with being a prayer for intercession, it is also used informally as a devotional prayer. The Hail Mary is not technically a prayer to Mary, but the request that Mary—along with others among the *communion of saints—intercede in prayer to God, on behalf of those who made their petitions known to Mary.

hands, laying on of. The act of placing hands on another person in order to bless them. Jesus blessed people by laying hands on them (e.g., Mark 10:16), and the *disciples laid hands on people as well, which empowered them (e.g., Acts 6:5-6). Throughout church history, the laying on of hands has occurred for the sake of *blessing, *healing, *commissioning, and ordaining people.

healing. The restoration of health to those who have been challenged physically by illness, injury, or bondage of some sort. Healing may also apply to spiritual, emotional, relational, and other challenges that cause misery and bondage in life. In *Scripture, God is the great healer and may heal people through the prayers of individuals or groups of individuals. However, healing is not described as an entitlement in Scripture, but a gracious gift that God may grant, which spiritually encourages as well as heals us.

healing, faith. A ministry specifically devoted to healing. Such ministries are thought to be heightened expressions of *faith and *compassion toward those in great need of holistic restoration.

healing, gifts of. A special enabling of the Holy *Spirit that empowers believers to heal. Because biblical references are to "gifts" (rather than a "gift") of healing, the gifting may be occasional rather than ongoing.

helps, gift of. A special enabling of the Holy *Spirit that empowers believers to help others extraordinarily beyond their means, usually in helping others in tangible, neighborly ways.

"Here I am." A prayer confessing one's humble presence before God and willingness to serve him in any way. The phrase comes from Isaiah's response to God's call for a volunteer to minister: "Here am I; send me!" (Isaiah 6:8).

hesychasm. A mystical tradition of silent prayer (Gk., *hēsychia*, "quiet, stillness"). Hesychasm has been popular, for example, in Orthodox Church traditions, and focuses on stillness and inner prayer, resulting in a kind of mental ascesis, sometimes known as *quietism. The *Philokalia* (Gk., "love for what is beautiful or good") is a collection of Orthodox monastic texts that teach on hesychasm and other monastic practices, including the *Jesus Prayer. They also provide practical advice for holy living.

high church, low church. Post-Reformation references to churches that use a more formal or less formal approach to public *worship services. For example, churches that generally have a more sacramental approach and make regular use of processions, vestments, *liturgy, the Christian *calendar, and other *rites and *rituals (e.g., weekly *Eucharist, incense, bells) are sometimes described as high church (or high liturgy churches). The Catholic and Orthodox churches, which use great formality reminiscent of historic worship practices, are thought of as being high church, as well as some Lutheran, Reformed, and Anglican churches. On the other hand, churches that take great liberty (and experiment) with regard to how worship services are structured and executed, not being bound by historic church practices, are sometimes described as low church (or low liturgy churches). Although the designations "high church" and "low church" are considered somewhat old-fashioned, they serve a useful purpose in contrasting different worship styles.

higher life movement. A movement that emphasizes the need for Christians to live a "higher life" spiritually, subsequent to *conversion, since God wants to sanctify as well as justify believers. Influenced by the *holiness and Keswick movements, the higher life movement emphasizes the need for Christians to grow into a more mature state of spiritual and moral living.

holiness movement. A movement that emphasizes holiness and the spiritual experience of entire *sanctification, advanced by John Wesley in Great Britain and Charles Finney in the United States, during the eighteenth and nineteenth centuries. The holiness movement incorporated emphases from *pietism along with American revivalism. It is believed that, just as one may experience an instantaneous conversion, one may also experience entire sanctification through a second crisis experience, subsequent to conversion.

holiness spirituality. A type of spirituality that emphasizes holy living and its pursuit, usually conceived in terms of piety and moral living. Holiness—its pursuit and maturation—is considered a heightened expression of Christian spirituality. Emphasis is placed on discipleship, obedience to the *teachings of *Jesus Christ, and formation of the *fruit of the Spirit.

holistic spirituality. Spirituality that emphasizes holistic health through various means, including spiritual practices, such as *prayer and *devotions, or physical practices, such as diet, exercise, and medical interventions. Holistic health takes into account every aspect of a person's existence, including spiritual, physical, emotional, and relational attributes. Sometimes references to holistic spirituality are made generically, rather than to a specific health movement, referring to the breadth and depth of God's work in the lives of people.

holy. God is thought to be holy, transcendent, righteous, and wholly perfect in all ways (Isaiah 6:3), and believers are called to be holy as God is holy (1 Peter 1:16). In the NT, holiness is comparable to *Christlikeness—becoming more and more like *Jesus Christ. Christians in church history differ with regard to the degree to which people cooperate with God in becoming holy, and the degree to which people can become holy. Historically, Catholic and Orthodox Churches have been hopeful regarding the degree to which people may become holy, and they consider it the responsibility of Christians to cooperate with God's *grace in the process of *sanctification. The Lutheran and Reformed churches have focused more on the challenges of *sin and believers' need to rely on God's initiative in becoming more holy. Later Pietist and Methodist Protestants reasserted the importance of holy living, the call to all Christians to love God and others, and that God's *Spirit enables such growth through participation in various spiritual practices, *spiritual exercises, and *spiritual disciplines.

holy day. A special day with religious significance (e.g., *Christmas, *Easter). The term has been shortened to *holiday* in contemporary usage. Holy days are important for the *spiritual discipline of *celebration, rejoicing for the blessings given by God. Holy days are liturgically listed in Christian calendars (*see* calendar, Christian). For example, Catholic and Orthodox churches observe many holy days (called *feast days by the

Orthodox), such as Epiphany, Ascension, and the Assumption of the Blessed Virgin Mary. Holy days/feast days usually mark major events in the life of *Jesus and the *saints.

Holy Spirit. *See* Spirit, Holy.

Holy Week. The week between the end of *Lent and the beginning of *Easter (or Pascha), which commemorates the events of the days leading up to *Jesus Christ's death and resurrection. For many Christians and churches, this week includes Palm Sunday, marking Jesus' triumphal entrance into Jerusalem, the Last Supper and Jesus' institution of *Communion on Holy Thursday, and the crucifixion of Jesus on Good Friday (or Holy Friday). The entire week serves as a time for spiritual remembrance, *encouragement, and *celebration.

hope. Positive expectancy that God ultimately controls the future. It includes both the act of hoping and the object (or end) for which one hopes. Christian hope primarily has to do with hope in God, which brings confidence both for present and future living (e.g., *resurrection, *eternal life). Hope is emphasized along with *faith and *love (1 Corinthians 13:13), and historically has been considered, along with faith and love, one of the prime theological virtues (*see* virtues, theological). Spiritually, hope serves to reassure Christians in this life, contributing to their faithful love and witness as well as optimism with regard to the degree to which God wants to transform people, individually and collectively.

hospitality. Welcoming and providing for others, including care for their spiritual well-being. Hospitality is considered a *virtue, and it encourages compassion and unity among people (e.g., Romans 12:13). Hospitality may be as simple as welcoming people to one's home, or welcoming people into one's church, especially those who are neglected, marginalized, or oppressed (e.g., Luke 14:13). Hospitality is considered important for ecumenical spirituality and for interfaith relations (*see* ecumenism); one never knows the spiritual significance of one's hospitality (Hebrews 13:2).

hourly prayer. A prayer *experience when one sets an hourly prompt to remind oneself to pray. Regular prayer times throughout the day reflect advice from the apostle Paul, who encouraged Christians to "pray without ceasing" (1 Thessalonians 5:17). Hourly prayer may include praying the *Hours.

Hours (canonical Hours, liturgy of the Hours). Specific times spaced throughout the day that are set aside for prayer. These typically include Lauds, Prime, Terce, Sext, None, *Vespers, and *Compline. Lauds is the first office of the day, traditionally prayed or chanted at daybreak, followed by the shorter Hours: Prime (practiced at 6:00 a.m.), Terce (9:00 a.m.), Sext (noon), None (3:00 p.m.), Vespers (6:00 p.m.), and Compline (night). Sometimes Lauds and Prime are combined. Among these Hours, Lauds and Vespers are primary, which both clergy and laity are expected to practice in high liturgy traditions. The Hours are also referred to as offices.

human, humanity. The final creation attested in Genesis 1. People are created in the *image of God (Genesis 1:27); the image of God is the central characteristic that distinguishes a Christian from a non-Christian view of humanity. People possess many qualities that may be observed and studied, but Christians do not think people can be fully understood without considering their spiritual nature, especially in relationship to God. Scripture analyzes humanity in various ways. Sometimes humans are described as consisting of a body and *soul (e.g., Matthew 10:28), sometimes as having a body, soul, and spirit (e.g., 1 Thessalonians 5:23), and sometimes as being a unified individual consisting of multiple dimensions. Regardless, spirituality remains at the core of who people are and of how they ought to live. However, people are not solitary. They exist as men and women, and they exist in community of various sorts. Gender may influence an individual's spirituality. Likewise, community—in its various manifestations—may influence an individual's spirituality as well as the spirituality of a group of individuals. Consideration of people's communal spirituality is as important to consider as their individual uniqueness. Finally, the behavioral sciences have provided constructive insights both into who people are and into who they are spiritually.

humility. The character of rightly understanding one's place in the world, especially in relationship to God, and not drawing attention to oneself unnecessarily. Humility is thought to be helpful for spirituality, since it may help people to be more God-focused than self-focused. Interestingly, humility was not considered a *virtue in Hellenistic culture, since it was caricatured as being passive and weak. Christianity, however, uplifted humility as a prime virtue, especially in relationship to God, reflective of *Jesus Christ, and beneficial for spiritual growth.

humor. That which is considered funny and amusing. Although *Scripture does not specifically talk about it, humor can aid people in preparing themselves—mentally, emotionally, and in other ways—for spiritual matters. There is no reason to think that spirituality must always be serious and lacking in humor. On the contrary, humor may be used to facilitate spiritual teachings, exercises, and disciplines.

hymns. Lyrics and *music intended for the *worship of God and the spiritual building up of people. In *Scripture, hymns are sung in public worship and are associated with *psalms and "spiritual songs" (Ephesians 5:19; Colossians 3:16; *see* song, spiritual). Throughout church history, hymns were written and sung by Christians, for example, Ephrem the Syrian (fourth century). Today hymns are sometimes identified with older hymnody, often using antiquated English phraseology; however, hymnody covers a much broader time frame, including contemporary lyrics and music sung in choruses.

I

icon. Stylized paintings visually expressing divine truth and the spiritual presence of *Jesus Christ and the *saints. Icons are characteristic of the Eastern Orthodox Church, where they are used in corporate and individual *worship. Devotionally, they aid people in meditating on God and spiritual realities. Icons (Gk., *eikōn*, "image") first appeared in the early church. Use of icons became a topic of debate between Eastern and Western churches because of the fear of idolatry. Eventually accusations of heresy were ameliorated at the Second Council of Nicaea in the eighth century, when a more nuanced understanding of iconographical use was reached, and the difference between idols and symbols, as well as worship and veneration, was achieved, largely through the efforts of John of Damascus.

icon prayer. Meditative prayer focused on an icon or other symbol of *faith. The goal is often to consume one's thoughts with the icon in order to *experience God in wholeness.

Ignatian spirituality. A disciplined form of spirituality established by Ignatius of Loyola, founder of the Jesuits, in the sixteenth century. Ignatian spirituality differs from other forms (such as *Carmelite or *Benedictine spirituality) in that it emphasizes detachment from worldly desires but not physical removal from society. Ignatian spirituality, therefore, is a form of spirituality for the working person who wishes to remain active in society. It emphasizes disciplined spiritual practices, such as the daily *examen, and retreats in order to discern God's will and to reshape one's desires so that *love of God is superior over all other loves. Ignatius put great emphasis on the need for Christians to make wise, disciplined choices that subdue their worldly attachments and promote God's greater glory. *See also* spiritual exercises of Ignatius.

ignorance, spiritual. A lack of knowledge or understanding with regard to spiritual matters. Ignorance can be an impediment to spirituality, especially due to people's ignorance of God and the *gospel. Ignorance does not excuse one from culpability of sin (e.g., Romans 1:18-20).

illumination. Divinely given insight and understanding. God is thought to give illumination to people, especially about spiritual matters. Martin Luther's conception of illumination involved the enlightenment people receive, especially regarding the *gospel message of *salvation (e.g., John 1:9; Ephesians 1:18).

image, imagery. A visualization that aids understanding and growth, especially with regard to spiritual matters. Images may be literal pictures or artwork; they may also be ideas, symbols, and *stories. There are many images Christians have used as spiritual aids: images from *Scripture, images from church history, images from other religious traditions, and creative contemporary images. Specific images may be found in Christian *art and *iconography.

image of God (Lat., *imago Dei*). The attribution or representation in which all people are created, reflective of God. Historically, Christians have considered the "image and likeness of God" (Genesis 1:26) to be the unique characteristic of *humanity, distinguishing them as superior to the rest of God's creation. The image (or visualization) of God may include more, but cannot include less, than the spiritual nature of humanity, by which humans relate with God and others. Although *Scripture does not explicitly describe what the image of God is, Christians have described it as including spirituality, rationality, choice, actions, morality, and relationality. Certainly there are other ways to understand the nature of humanity, and new understandings continue to arise. But the spiritual nature of people and their relationship with God are inextricably bound up with who they are.

imagination, spiritual. An ability to think creatively especially about spiritual matters. *Scripture refers to imagination negatively, as making up untruths (Acts 17:29), but imagination also has to do with being creative and resourceful. God enables people to be innovative in understanding and applying things about Christian spirituality through imagination.

imitation of Christ. The practice of imitating by God's *grace the beliefs, values, and practices of *Jesus Christ. The followers of Christ were first called "Christians" in the city of Antioch (Acts 11:26) because they followed the life and teachings of Christ. In other words, they sought, by the aid of divine grace, to imitate Christ. In the fifteenth century, Thomas à Kempis wrote *The Imitation of Christ*, which functioned as a devotional handbook for Christians, reflective of his support of the *Devotio Moderna* movement. Thomas provided helpful counsels and directives for nurturing an individual's spiritual or "interior life." Such nurture could be accomplished by any Christian, coupled with faithful participation in the church's various means of grace (*see* grace, means of), especially the *sacrament of the *Eucharist.

imprecatory prayer. Prayers for withstanding and overcoming one's enemies, who are also thought to be the enemies of God. In the *Psalms, prayers were offered to God for the judgment and destruction of opponents of God and those who prayed.

Imprecate means to curse or invoke *evil, judgment, and destruction on others. For example, Psalm 69:27-28 says: "Add guilt to their guilt; may they have no acquittal from you. Let them be blotted out of the book of the living; let them not be enrolled among the righteous." Although Jesus commanded his followers to love their enemies (Matthew 5:44), Christians offer imprecatory prayers when it is believed that both God and they are religiously opposed, treated unjustly, or persecuted.

in Christ. Being spiritually united with Christ. "In Christ" is the primary way the apostle Paul describes Christians (e.g., Romans 8:1; Galatians 3:26-28). The repetitive mention of those who are "in Christ" implies that Christians are identified by their *union with Jesus Christ. They share in his death and *resurrection, as well as in the nature of Christians as "followers" of Christ. If people are in Christ, then they engage in spiritual activities that bring them into a deeper union with Christ.

incarnation. The doctrine of *Jesus Christ's full divinity and full humanity, as God becoming embodied in flesh (Lat., *incarnatio*, "incarnation, embodiment"). Originally, the incarnation represented the *mystery that Jesus, who is divine (Heb., *ʿimmānûʾēl*, "God is with us"), became embodied in finite, human flesh, or "enfleshed." Conceived by the Holy *Spirit and born of the Virgin *Mary, Jesus—who in Christian understanding is the second person of the *Trinity—voluntarily humbled himself in order to become human, to live among people, and to save them from their *sins through his death and resurrection. Theologically the word is used to describe how spiritual realities in life may be experienced through physical means. Other examples include the elements of the *sacraments (i.e., *water, *bread, *wine). Any physical object, by God's *grace, may aid people spiritually (e.g., an *icon, *rosary, or prayer rope). In ministry, incarnational language has been used to describe a lifestyle that "embodies" the *gospel (set in contrast to vocal proclamations of the gospel). Incarnational living emphasizes how care for the physical well-being of others may be as relevant and effective in loving others as care for them spiritually.

inclusive-language prayers. Prayers that use inclusive language (or non-male-exclusive) language in reference to people, and even to God. God is revealed in *Scripture primarily using male-oriented language because humans must rely on symbolic, analogical, and metaphorical language to describe God. However, it is believed that God, who is spirit, ultimately transcends any finite and human absolute description. Inclusive-language prayers are thought to be especially important when referring to people because such prayers prevent anyone from being linguistically omitted, especially in public prayers. Christians and churches may use prayers, *liturgies, *songs, and other materials in public *worship that are inclusive so that all people will feel welcome and valued in the worship experience. Some Christians think it is important, and even necessary, to refer to God using only inclusive language. For example, people may pray to God, to God their Parent, or to God their Father and Mother, rather than referring to God only as Father.

infused prayer. A *mystical, contemplative prayer, during which it is believed the mind becomes entirely focused on God. Infused *contemplation is said to be the natural course prayer takes after vocal prayer, *meditation, affective prayer, and prayer of simplicity. The preceding stages of prayer are purgative (*see* purification), whereas infused prayers of contemplation are seen as the beginning of true *union with God—the mystical phase of union (or communion) with God.

inner light. The light of God, which is given to reveal truth, and guide people in their lives and ministries, especially associated with the presence and work of the Holy *Spirit. *Jesus Christ described himself as "the light of the world" (John 8:12), and God's Spirit continues as that light. The Society of Friends (Quakers) emphasizes the inner light (or inner voice) of God's Spirit for all dimensions of adherents' spiritual lives as well as for *salvation.

intellect. *See* reason.

intercession. Prayer on behalf of others, for individuals or groups of individuals. *Scripture exhorts people to pray for rulers as well as for one's enemies (e.g., Matthew 5:44). Intercessory prayer may be made for the spiritual and physical needs of others, for their deliverance from difficulties and enemies, and for intervention during other crises. *Jesus interceded for his *disciples, and the Holy *Spirit continues to intercede for us (Romans 8:26-27). Intercession is thought to be one of the most common types of prayer, which benefits the one who prays in addition to those for whom intercessory prayer is made. Catholic and Orthodox Christians believe that the *communion of saints, including *Mary the mother of Jesus, continue to intercede on behalf of those who live on earth.

interreligious prayer (or interfaith prayer). Prayer with people from different religious or faith traditions. Interreligious prayer often occurs in pluralistic contexts, for example, at community meetings, public prayer breakfasts, or public days of prayer.

J

Jesus Christ. The person who, as God incarnate, was born, lived, died, and was resurrected as "the anointed" one (Heb., *māšîaḥ*; Gk., *Christos*)—the Messiah, the Christ—for the *salvation of *humanity. Theologically, Jesus is considered the second person of the *Trinity, who voluntarily humbled himself and became human, that is, incarnate. In becoming incarnate, Jesus did more than provide for people's salvation; he also revealed more about God than had previously been known, especially more personal knowledge about God (e.g., John 1:18; 14:7-11). Now Jesus serves as an *intercessor who empathizes with our human frailties (Hebrews 4:14-16), and he will be a final and just judge of humanity in the end times (John 5:22-27). First John 3:8 also talks about how Jesus overcomes the work of *demons so that Christians need not fear the possession of demonic powers on them. Most importantly, for the sake of spirituality, Jesus exemplified a model or pattern for how Christians ought to live, spiritually, ethically, ministerially, and other ways (1 Peter 2:21; 1 John 2:6). Thus, Jesus serves as a spiritual as well as an ethical and ministerial role model for Christians. In Scripture, the followers of Jesus became known as "Christians"—those who are like Christ (see Acts 11:26). By the grace of God, Christians endeavor to become Christlike in pursuit of holy living.

Jesus, in the name of. The authoritative claim to pray or perform acts of ministry "in the name of Jesus." Jesus gave his
followers authority to proclaim the *gospel, cast out *demons,
and to perform other signs and wonders. After *Pentecost,
new believers were baptized "in the name of Jesus Christ"
(Acts 2:38). Thereafter, Christians pray in the name of Jesus,
usually in their *benedictions, and *liturgy regularly appeals
to the name of Jesus, especially for the *sacraments. In *prayer,
the name of Jesus is significant because of the power that is associated with the proper use of his name. Invoking the name
of Jesus is correlated with *healings, *exorcisms, freedom from
*sin, freedom from addiction, and closer intimacy with God.
In some devotional prayers, the name of Jesus is the focus of
the prayer, as in the *Jesus Prayer. Some simply repeat the
name of Jesus during times of distress in order to receive comfort and *encouragement.

Jesus Prayer (Prayer to Jesus). An ancient prayer based on Matthew 20:30-31 and Luke 18:13. Though the prayer is found with
various forms, a common version is: "Lord Jesus Christ, Son of
God, have mercy on me, a sinner." Other versions abbreviate
the prayer, removing "Son of God" and "a sinner," or removing
all but "Lord have mercy." The prayer is used to bring *silence,
introspection, and tranquility, with the intention of moving
the believer from a prayer of the mind to a prayer of the heart.
The Jesus Prayer continues to be an important spiritual practice
among Orthodox Christians. It is often prayed with a prayer
rope or bracelet, simply as a means of focusing on the prayer.

journal, spiritual. Journaling used as a means for expressing one's
innermost spiritual self, aspirations, and prayers. Journaling
helps some people gain greater spiritual insight, because it encourages them to express their thoughts and feelings about God.

journaling prayers. Writing out one's prayers in a diary-like
fashion. This can follow any number of other forms of prayer,
except that they are written. One unique use of journaling is to
record intercessory prayers, marking them as they are prayed
for again, and highlighting them when they are answered.

journey, spiritual. An image of travel or pilgrimage used for
gaining greater understanding about the ups and downs of

one's spiritual life. Many find it helpful to reflect on their spiritual past, present, and future as part of a process that includes challenges, successes, and a final goal that inspires perseverance. The most famous use of this journey imagery occurs in John Bunyan's *Pilgrim's Progress. See also* pilgrimage.

joy. The state of being delighted and happy, especially for spiritual reasons. *Scripture describes joy as a result of God's Holy *Spirit at work in the lives of believers, and as such is a sign of spirituality. The apostle Paul described joy as one of the *fruits of the Spirit.

justice. That which has to do with what is right and fair, especially understood as a religious and spiritual obligation. There are many ways that the word *justice* (Gk., *dikaiosynē*) is used in *Scripture. First and foremost, justice is used to describe God and God's relations with people (e.g., Deuteronomy 32:4). Likewise, God commands people to be just and to advocate on behalf of those treated unjustly (e.g., Leviticus 19:15). For some Christians, the pursuit of justice—individually and socially—represents the height of spirituality, reflective of an *activist understanding of biblical teachings.

justification. A doctrine derived from the apostle Paul's epistles, the background of the doctrine of justification is a judicial action by which a person's legal status is declared or made righteous. While the precise theological meaning of justification is much debated, it is God's action based on the atoning death of *Jesus Christ. In some Protestant understandings, justification (Gk., *dikaioō*) is understood as a righteousness imputed to believers; it is "as if" they are now righteous from God's perspective. It is the gift of God, and not the result of human effort or merit (Ephesians 2:8). This doctrine is a crucial distinctive of the Protestant Reformation, which broadly distinguishes God's reckoning, or declaring, sinners righteous from any notion of infused righteousness. More recently Lutheran and Catholic scholars have come closer in their understanding of the Pauline doctrine of justification. Most Protestants will make a careful distinction between justification and *sanctification, with the latter referring the transformative growth into *Christlikeness that follows justification.

K

kenosis. The self-emptying of the Son of God in becoming human. Use of the word *kenōsis* (Gk., "emptying") is derived from Philippians 2:7 in order to describe Christ's voluntary self-humbling in becoming incarnate. Although Christians have differing views of the precise nature of this kenosis, they agree that Jesus serves as a model for how Christians are to live spiritually, ethically, and ministerially. They should reflect Jesus' voluntary and humble setting aside of privilege in their *spiritual formation, their pursuit of *holiness, and their leadership.

kingdom of God, kingdom of heaven. The in-breaking reign of God that characterized the message and ministry of *Jesus Christ. In the Gospels Jesus sometimes refers to the kingdom as being "near" (Matthew 3:2; Luke 21:31) or "come upon you" (Matthew 12:28; Luke 11:20) or even "among you" (Luke 17:21). The kingdom metaphor is a rich symbol of the reign of God being manifest in Jesus. It is not identified with this world and is not synonymous with the *church, which bears witness to the kingdom. One day the kingdom of God will visibly embrace all of creation.

kiss, holy. A greeting encouraged by Paul in Romans 16:16 and other passages. The kiss was a common greeting in the early church and indicated a form of social as well as religious acceptance. Christians from different sociocultural contexts vary in their spiritually significant expressions of physical touch and may use alternative forms, including handshakes and hugs. Though the holy kiss is not literally practiced in many Western churches, the concept of showing someone filial love through physical touch can be a healing and welcoming act. When we embrace someone who needs affirmation, we minister to them as Christ would. Orthodox Christians often greet one another with three kisses (in honor of the *Trinity) on the cheek.

kneeling. *See* prayer positions.

knowledge, gift of. A special enabling of the Holy *Spirit that empowers believers with knowledge beyond their human abilities. It may involve general knowledge, contemporaneous knowledge of someone else's situation or struggle (so that the person given the knowledge may give prayer or aid), or extraordinary discovery, integration, application, or *teaching of biblical knowledge.

koinōnia. See fellowship.

L

labyrinth. A complex pattern, usually designed on the ground or on the floor of a church, which provides a single path to the center of the pattern. Prayerfully or mindfully traveling the course of the labyrinth helps people focus spiritually. The tradition of labyrinths goes back to ancient Greece, but in medieval times labyrinths increasingly appeared in Christian church contexts. Eventually, labyrinths were used as spiritual aids for the sake of focusing on God or other religious exercises, while walking (or crawling) to the center of the pattern. A famous labyrinth used for spiritual concentration is located in the Chartres Cathedral in France.

ladder, spiritual. An image derived from Jacob's ladder (Genesis 28) used to describe progressive spiritual growth. For most Christian traditions the spiritual ladder leads from *conversion to a higher form of spirituality, usually culminating in *love. Typically, the spiritual ladder is ascended through prayer, since the purpose of the ladder is to bring the believer closer to God. *The Ladder of Ascent*, by John Climacus, is a classic text on this topic.

lament. A sorrowful prayer or song that includes mourning or complaining to God about the circumstances of life. The *Psalms contain many prayers of individual and corporate lament, and the entire book of Lamentations consists of poetic prayers, which include *petitions for consolation as well as deliverance.

law. The rules commanded by God, pertaining to civil, criminal, social, and spiritual life. Although people are accountable to the laws of God for sins they commit, God has graciously provided atonement for their sin through *Jesus Christ. In presenting the *gospel message of *salvation, Jesus said that he did not come to "abolish" the law but to "fulfill" it (Matthew 5:17).

During the Protestant Reformation, Martin Luther said that the law served two uses: to convict people of *sin and to maintain civil order. John Calvin added a third use of the law to provide moral guidance for Christian living.

lectio divina. A method of reading *Scripture, rooted in the concept that God is present in the words of Scripture, speaking through them. *Lectio* (Lat.) means "reading," and *divina* (Lat.) means "divine, sacred," and together they refer to the divine, sacred, or spiritual reading of Scripture. Lectio divina, which emphasizes reading from the heart, is distinct from more scholastic approaches to Scripture reading, which emphasize studying with the mind. In the twelfth century, Guigo II first articulated the four stages of lectio divina. First, reading (*lectio*) involves the perusal of a short passage repeatedly (perhaps three times). The goal is to become familiar with the text without thinking about what it means. The text is read in various ways by pausing after certain words or sentences, in order to change the emphasis in the passage. Through reading the text in multiple, varying ways, the text is impressed on the reader's mind. Second, *meditation (Lat., *meditatio*) reflects on and ponders the text, which at this point is familiar to the reader. After looking at the text from every angle, the reader sits in silence, meditating on the text. Unlike scholastic readings, the goal of this stage is not to get at the original meaning of the text, but to think about what God is saying to the reader through the text. Third, prayer (Lat., *oratio*) occurs in dialogue with God. Depending on the outcome of *meditatio*, the reader may respond in a number of ways: thanksgiving, questions, *praise, words of intimacy. Prayer is spontaneous, and so it has no prescribed formula. Since the ultimate goal of lectio divina is closeness with God, this stage begins the movement from the mind to the heart, from self-centered existence to God-centered existence, from the text to God. In the meditative stage, the reader may hear God's voice; in the prayerful stage, the reader responds to God's voice. Fourth, *contemplation (Lat., *contemplatio*) enables one to rest in the presence of God. It is the simplest stage, and is more heartfelt than intellectual. After having become familiar with the scriptural passage and dialoguing with God, one rests in *silence, enjoying the depth of intimacy with God. There is no goal in contemplation except rest and enjoyment. Some Christians add a fifth stage of *incarnation (Lat., *incarnatio*), which emphasizes personal application (or embodiment) of Scripture. Since no one can enter the presence of God without being changed, when one concludes lectio divina the next step is to go and act on whatever God has revealed. This fifth stage may be thought to contradict the purpose of lectio divina, however, which emphasizes *being* in God's presence rather than *doing*.

lectionary. A prescribed order of biblical passages used for *preaching, usually so that the whole of *Scripture is preached over a multiyear period. The lectionary avoids preaching that omits or diminishes parts of Scripture. Churches that use lectionaries consider them a part of their *liturgy and *worship, promoting a holistic emphasis on Scripture and spirituality.

Lent. The period of spiritual preparation before *Easter. Lent (Old Eng., "spring") begins with Ash Wednesday in Catholic churches and with Pure Monday in Orthodox churches. Lent lasts forty days, symbolic of Jesus' *fasting and *prayer in the desert for the same number of days (Matthew 4:1-11). The Lenten season provides the opportunity for spiritual reflection on one's sins and making repentance for them. Traditionally, Catholics usually fast from one food item of individual choice during Lent, while Orthodox Christians submit to a common fast from meat, dairy, wine, and oil. In contemporary times, Christians from all church traditions have become creative in their spiritual observance of Lent, possibly abstaining from certain foods and activities or adding new spiritual disciplines or ministries as expressions of *love to God and others.

liberation. The setting free of those who are in bondage, slavery, or some kind of unjust captivity, including spiritual liberation. God momentously liberated the Israelites from the bondage of slavery in Egypt, and *Jesus Christ described his ministry by saying: "He [God] has sent me to proclaim release to the captives and recovery of sight to the blind, to let the oppressed go free" (Luke 4:18). In the twentieth century, liberation theologians have talked about the need to liberate people spiritually from their bondage to sin and death, and also to liberate them from material forms of systemic oppression, since spiritual and physical bondage are interconnected. *See also* justice.

listening prayer. Prayer that emphasizes listening to God rather than speaking to God. Listening prayer is a dialogical form of prayer that asks God a question and then awaits a response. It differs from *hesychasm and *quietism in that listening prayer usually begins with a specific request or question, whereas the purpose hesychasm and quietism is to focus on God without requests.

litany. A formal and prescribed corporate prayer of *petition. Litanies originated as processional prayers, sometimes involve a call-and-response format. A clergy, elder, or deacon makes a supplication to God; the congregation or choir responds to the prayer with a scripted form of assent. Litanies are typically used in Catholic and Orthodox churches, though some Protestant churches have incorporated litanies into their liturgies.

liturgical spirituality. A type of spirituality that emphasizes public *worship, liturgy, and the centrality of the *sacraments. Participation in liturgy is considered a heightened expression of Christian spirituality. An example would be a spirituality that is deeply shaped and influenced by the *Book of Common Prayer.

liturgical year. *See* calendar, Christian.

liturgy. The order of rites and rituals performed during regular Christian gatherings and on *holy days. Liturgies are typically scripted. In high liturgy traditions, the script is detailed and consistent with the songs, *Scripture readings, and themes determined for each week on an annual or three-year *lectionary cycle. Some high-liturgy (*high church) traditions distinguish between proper and ordinary (or common) liturgy. In low-liturgy (or low church) traditions, the script is less detailed, providing only a weekly template for gatherings. In these low-liturgy traditions, the liturgy is usually referred to as an order of service, since the only consistent element is the order in which the liturgical elements are performed. Even the most informal service may follow a basic liturgical form of order: a service may begin with prayer, followed by worship songs, announcements, a sermon (or homily), additional worship songs, and a closing prayer. For Christian spirituality, liturgy is important for two reasons. First, it creates a sense of expectation, training believers to anticipate certain spiritual events. If used correctly, this anticipation then allows believers to prepare mentally and emotionally to engage in that particular form of *worship. Second, through repetition, liturgy trains the congregation to view certain practices as important. In evangelical traditions, musical worship and sermons are emphasized through the prominence and time allotted to them in the liturgical order of worship, whereas other traditions give more prominence to Scripture reading, *Eucharist, *fellowship time, or *prayer. In high liturgical traditions, by scripting not only the order of the liturgy but also the lectionary topics for each week, a consistency is created across multiple congregations. Liturgy has the added benefit of worship entering into the consensus of a balanced tradition, whereby Scripture and themes of the church year are covered systematically. In contexts where choice is an option, Christians often feel drawn to either high or low liturgy churches based on which form of worship most effectively ministers to them spiritually or enhances their worship.

"Lord have mercy." A common prayer among Christians most often uttered as a plea for God's intervention in matters that are considered beyond human capacity to alter or help. *See also* Jesus Prayer.

Lord's Prayer. The well-loved Christian prayer derived from Jesus' instruction to his disciples on how to pray (Matthew 6:9-13; Luke 11:2-4). There exist several versions of the Lord's Prayer, each adding to or modifying the wording, but essentially faithful to the Gospel versions. A popular English-language version of the Lord's Prayer dates back to the Roman Catholic Church, including a benediction, found in the Anglican *Book of Common Prayer. The prayer appears as follows:

> Our Father who art in heaven, hallowed be thy name.
>> Thy kingdom come.
>> Thy will be done on earth as it is in heaven.
>> Give us this day our daily bread, and forgive us our trespasses, as we forgive those who trespass against us, and lead us not into temptation, but deliver us from evil.

For thine is the kingdom, and the power, and the glory, for ever and ever.

Amen.

A well-known variation in the Lord's Prayer has to do with use of the words "debts" and "debtors," instead of the words "trespasses" and "those who trespass." The former words reflect Matthew's symbolic use of debtors with regard to sin, whereas Luke spoke more directly about the forgiveness of sins. Over time, various words were used in English translations of *Scripture, and the earliest translators such as William Tyndale used the word "trespasses" (ca. 1526). In 1611, the King James Version reinstated the word "debtors," which explains in part the ongoing differences in wording. Contemporary ecumenical versions of the Lord's Prayer focus on sins. For example, a contemporary English-language version of the Lord's Prayer was formulated by the 1988 English Language Liturgical Consultation:

Our Father in heaven, hallowed be your name, your kingdom come, your will be done, on earth as in heaven.

Give us today our daily bread.

Forgive us our sins as we forgive those who sin against us.

Save us from the time of trial and deliver us from evil.

For the kingdom, the power, and the glory are yours now and for ever.

Amen.

Although there exist many ways of understanding the Lord's Prayer, it is generally thought to contain—at least within its most common versions—an introduction, seven petitions, and a doxology. The seven petitions may be summarized as follows, using the English Language Liturgical Consultation's version of the Lord's Prayer:

1. Hallowed be your name.

2. Your kingdom come.

3. Your will be done.

4. Give us today our daily bread.

5. Forgive us our sins as we forgive those who sin against us.

6. Save us from the time of trial.

7. Deliver us from evil.

All variations of the Lord's Prayer begin with the words "Our Father." As such, Catholics refer to the prayer as the *Our Father. Jesus' paternal reference to God as Father models a more personal and intimate relationship with God than had been characteristic of previous prayers to God in Scripture. Christians concerned about using inclusive language in reference to God may not use the name "Father" in their recitation of the Lord's Prayer. The Lord's Prayer has been used for centuries by Christians as the consummate model of prayer, both for personal and public use. Some Christians use the Lord's Prayer as a holistic guide for their prayer lives, and model their prayers after it. They may also use the Lord's Prayer as a *benediction for either personal or public prayers. In public worship, the Lord's Prayer is the most commonly quoted prayer from Scripture, regardless of the particular version that is used. The Lord's Prayer may be spoken as a *blessing on almost any hallowed occasion, whether it be a dedication, wedding, or funeral.

Lord's Supper. The Christian sacramental practice of eating *bread and drinking *wine. The practice reflects *Jesus Christ's last supper with his disciples, which is mentioned in all four Gospels (Matthew 26:17-30; Mark 14:12-26; Luke 22:7-39; cf. John 21:20). The *sacrament of the Lord's Supper, or Holy Supper, is also known as the *Eucharist, *Communion, and *Mass. Eucharist (Gk., *eucharistia*) means to give "thanks" or "good grace," and the name reflects the fact that Jesus gave thanks for the bread and wine before distributing them to his *disciples. Communion, or Holy Communion, conveys the communing that took place between Jesus and his disciples, and ongoing communion between Jesus and contemporary participants in the sacrament. Mass means the "dismissal" or culmination of the sacramental service, and has also come to signify God's "mission" for Christians in the world. There are different Christian views of the Lord's Supper, just as there are different views of the sacraments. How one understands the sacraments in general influences how one specifically understands the Lord's Supper. Some Protestants emphasize the spiritual, albeit real, presence of Jesus Christ, emphasizing that participants receive divine *grace in ways that they would not otherwise receive; other Protestants emphasize the symbolic nature of the Lord's Supper, emphasizing that participants figuratively remember Jesus' atonement as a memorial, and that divine grace is always available in the lives of believers. Catholics and Orthodox believe that Jesus was speaking literally, rather than spiritually or symbolically, when he gave thanks for the bread and wine. Thus every time priests give thanks for the bread and wine, the elements' essence miraculously become the body and blood of Jesus, while the accidents (e.g., taste, texture) remain the same. Sometimes grape juice, rather than wine (fermented grape juice), is preferred by church bodies that teach against the consumption of alcohol, as well as for the sake of those with alcoholic drinking problems. Since the Lord's Supper is considered a specific, formal means of grace (*see* grace, means of)—instituted by Jesus—participation in it by believers is considered vital for their spiritual development. Whether by the reception of uniquely given grace or by faithful remembrance of the grace always available to believers, participation in the Lord's Supper is recommended as a regular *worship practice (1 Corinthians 11:23-26).

Lordship of Jesus Christ. Jesus Christ's rule over the universe, generally, and more specifically, his rule over all aspects of an individual Christian's life. Jesus challenged the faithfulness of some followers, asking: "Why do you call me 'Lord, Lord,' and do not do what I tell you?" (Luke 6:46). Those described as living under the Lordship of *Jesus Christ are thought to have entirely consecrated themselves to a Christlike life.

love. A deep affection and commitment; from a Christian perspective, love is the highest *virtue. In *Scripture, love is a primary attribute of God (1 John 4:8, 16), and God graciously demonstrates love to people by creating and redeeming them. In response, love represents the greatest expression one can have toward God, toward oneself, and toward others. *Jesus Christ said that the greatest commandment, which summed up all "the law and the prophets," had to do with loving God with one's whole heart, *soul, mind, and strength, and loving one's neighbor as one loves oneself (Matthew 22:40; Mark 12:28-31). As God first loved the world by giving Jesus to die on the cross for our salvation (1 John 4:19), Christians are called to follow Jesus' example, living a self-sacrificial life for the sake of others. Scripture uses several words that are translated as "love," most often *philia* and *agapē*. *Philia* conveys a filial, brotherly or sisterly love, and *agapē* conveys an unconditional love. Although *philia* and *agapē* are sometimes used interchangeably in the NT, *agapē* is generally considered the qualitatively superior expression of love. *Agapē* is most often associated with God's love for people. *Eros* is another Greek word translated as love; it is not explicitly mentioned in Scripture, but it represents romantic love (e.g., Song of Songs). Love is considered both a *fruit of the Spirit as well as a virtuous way of living, which needs cultivation. *See also* virtues, theological.

love, disinterested. Love that is not thought to be motivated by self-interest, considered especially descriptive of Christian love. Disinterested love is thought to be a higher form of love for God and others over against love done for the sake of getting something in return. Spiritually, Christians ought to love God and to pursue their spiritual growth for its intrinsic good, with a sense of abandonment or *detachment from self-interest, rather than for advantages one may receive only in this life.

love feast (or *agapē* feast). Religious meals associated with, but separate from, the *Eucharist. The tradition of love feasts is found in 1 Corinthians 11, where Paul rebukes the church for abuses in relation to communal meals. Eventually, love feasts fell out of favor within churches, but were renovated by Moravians, Methodists, and others in the eighteenth century. Love feasts are practiced in various ways. For example, Methodists practice an informal liturgy for love feasts, which includes *hymns, *testimonies, a meal, *teaching, and other spiritual practices.

love, overflowing (Ger., *quellende Liebe*). The love of God that overflows in believers, making them loving and generous toward others. Martin Luther believed that God's love would overflow into people so that they would progressively become more spiritually mature and loving in service to others.

love, perfect. A biblical term used to describe a heightened state of Christian spirituality. First John 4:18 says: "There is no fear in love, but perfect love casts out fear; for fear has to do with punishment, and whoever fears has not reached perfection in love." Love is described as a *virtue that can be perfected to the extent of overcoming fear. Some Christians have understood the goal of *spiritual formation (and of *sanctification) as *perfection, or Christian perfection, achieved through *theosis, counsels of perfection (*see* perfection, counsels of), or other means of grace (*see* grace, means of).

low church. *See* high church, low church.

M

Magnificat. A canticle derived from the words of *Mary the mother of Jesus recorded in Luke 1:46-55. The song begins with her words "My soul magnifies the Lord" (Luke 1:46). It is used in liturgical traditions, and sung or recited for prayers and worship services. The canticle exemplifies Mary's spiritual *humility in submitting to God's will and her delight in serving God.

mapping a spiritual journey. The process of creating a visualization or timeline of one's spiritual journey that maps past blessings from God and one's spiritual progress. Mapping one's spiritual journal (*see* journal, spiritual) also charts failures and shortcomings, which can help one plan future spiritual growth.

Marian spirituality (or Marian devotion). Spirituality motivated by reverence and devotion to *Mary the mother of Jesus Christ. Catholic Christians believe that Mary did not die, but was assumed bodily into heaven and now lives among the *communion of saints, who intercede to God in prayer on behalf of those who are still alive on earth. As such, Christians now venerate Mary and request her intercession to God on behalf of their petitions. Thus Mary helps those who seek her spiritual assistance, heartening their reliance on God for their needs. Numerous advocates and societies have arisen in promoting Marian spirituality, such as Julian of Norwich (fourteenth century) and Thérèse of Lisieux (nineteenth century). Protestants honor Mary, not as an intercessor, but as a spiritual role model of humble obedience and servanthood.

marriage. The joining of a man and a woman in conjugal and spiritual union with one another. Marriage was instituted by God and involves a *covenant relationship, which embraces all aspects of life between two people. Scripture often uses marriage as an analogy for people's relationship with God. For example, God is said to have a marriage relationship with the people of Israel, and *Jesus Christ is bridegroom of the church (e.g., Revelation 19:7). Spiritually, Christians throughout church history have talked about their individual as well as collective relationship with God by using the analogy of marriage, especially the importance of fidelity to God and of the spiritual growth that occurs in covenantal relationship with God.

marriage, spiritual. A marriage based on emotional and spiritual but not sexual intimacy. Sometimes known as love without *sex, Christians in church history have entered into marriage for the sake of *spiritual formation rather than for procreation. In Catholicism, clergy enter into a kind of spiritual marriage when they take vows of *celibacy, as do other laypeople who take similar vows for the sake of serving God and others.

martyr. Bearing witness (Gk., *martyria*) to *Jesus Christ through the ultimate imitation of Jesus, sharing in his literal death. The deacon Stephen was the first follower of Jesus to be martyred (Acts 7). The witness aspect of martyrdom was important for early Christians, who followed the call to "take up their cross" both figuratively and literally (Matthew 16:24). Martyrs in the second century included Ignatius of Antioch and Justin Martyr. Many of them envisioned literal suffering for the sake of Jesus as part of the call to Christianity; however, they believed that there must be some purpose behind suffering. Martyrs were praised and sainted by Catholic and Orthodox Christians for their faithfulness in the face of death; the self-*sacrifice of martyrs was later emulated by individuals who led self-sacrificial lives, for example, living as *ascetic or *monastic Christians. Protestants have also venerated martyrs, for example, as found in *Foxe's Book of Martyrs*.

Mary. The mother of *Jesus. Throughout church history, Mary has figured significantly in the spiritual lives of Christians, believing that she resides among the *communion of saints, and intercedes to God on behalf of those who request her intercession. In Catholic and Orthodox churches, Mary is also known as the Blessed Virgin Mary, Blessed Mother, Panaghia (All-Holy One), and Theotokos (God-Bearer).

Mass (or Holy Mass). One of the names for the *sacrament celebrating *Jesus Christ's last supper with his *disciples. The term derives from *missa* (Lat., "dismissal"), communicating both the end of public *worship in which the sacrament is administered and the "mission" of Christians going forth in the world. Mass, or Holy Mass, is used in Catholic and some Protestant churches. *See also* Lord's Supper; Eucharist.

Matins. The morning prayer service, derived from the Latin word for "belonging to the morning." Matins is sometimes called Lauds (Lat., "praises") in Catholic churches, Orthros (Gk., "daybreak") in Orthodox churches, and Morning Prayer in Anglican churches. Traditionally, Matins was the last of four monastic night services, ending at dawn.

maturity, spiritual. The term sometimes used in *Scripture for describing the goal of Christlike character and behavior—of *godliness and *holiness (Ephesians 4:13-15). It includes spiritual understanding, *discernment, righteous living, and good works. Although the term suggests a completed state of existence, Christians talk about spiritual maturity more as a heightened awareness and continued growth in spirituality.

meditation. A deliberative practice during which a believer reflects on some spiritual *wisdom, whether found in *Scripture or in some other Christian writing, *song, or *art. Scripture talks about the importance of meditating on God, God's words, and the works of God, for example, God's creation. Psalm 1:1-2 says that people are "happy" who "meditate day and night" on God's words, law, and prophets. Meditation aids in praising and worshiping God, growing in *faith, understanding, and wisdom, and in obeying God. Teresa of Ávila considered meditation a preliminary practice before advancing to *contemplative prayer. The purpose of meditation is to fill the mind with thoughts about God rather than extraneous thoughts. *Lectio divina is a spiritual exercise, widely practiced, which centers on the meditation of Scripture. In *mysticism, meditation is the second stage—the illuminative stage—on the way to communing and achieving *union with God.

memorization. Committing to memory what has been read and learned, for the purpose of recall and spiritual benefit. *Scripture talks about the importance of remembering the words and works of God in the past, and of how they comfort, guide, and encourage us in the present (e.g., Psalm 119:11). Christians have long emphasized the importance of memorizing Scripture, along with other spiritually valuable literature and *songs, which makes it easier for them to meditate on God.

mendicant spirituality. A form of spirituality characterized by itinerant *preaching and begging by friars, who were traveling *monks. Mendicant (Lat., *mendicans*, "begging") orders arose at the turn of the thirteenth century in contrast to the sequestered monastic traditions of spirituality. Dominic of Caleruega gave leadership to the Dominican order, which excelled in preaching, apologetics, and scholastic theology; and Francis of Assisi gave leadership to Franciscan orders, which excelled in preaching, voluntary *poverty, care for the sick, and promotion of lay spirituality.

men's spirituality. Spirituality distinctive to men. There is no agreement among Christians with regard to whether there is spirituality distinctive to men, in contrast to women. But increasingly some emphasize the need to understand and promote spirituality for the specific character and needs of men, as well as for the specific character and needs of women. Especially after the rise of biblical feminist concerns, some Christians have identified gender challenges and concerns among men with regard to their understanding and pursuit of *spiritual formation. For example, consideration is given to biological and cultural differences. *See also* women's spirituality.

mental prayer. A silent prayer that emphasizes dialogical, *meditative, and *contemplative expressions. Catholics refer to mental prayer in contrast to vocal prayer (*see* prayer, vocal), which uses liturgical and spoken approaches with God. Teresa of Ávila advocated mental prayer as a kind of interior or mystical prayer, which seeks *perfection.

mentor, spiritual. One who gives spiritual, personal, and relational guidance to another individual over a prolonged period of time. Similar to a *spiritual director, a mentor is one who usually lives, works, or can communicate with other people often enough to mentor them on a regular basis. Of course, people can be mentored many ways as lay leaders and clergy. But spiritual mentoring focuses specifically on the spiritual well-being and growth of another person.

mind. The location of a person's ability to reason, which Christians consider to be part of God's good creation. People's minds and reasoning capacity have been identified with being created in the *image of God, and as significant for spiritual well-being. In *Scripture, *Jesus Christ added to the words of the *Shema, saying that one is to love God "with all your mind" (Mark 12:30). The apostle Paul says that Christians are to be transformed by the "renewing of your minds" (Romans 12:2), and elsewhere he exhorts them to let "the same mind be in you that was in Christ Jesus" (Philippians 2:5). To be sure, Scripture gives warning against letting one's mind supersede one's spirituality. Nevertheless, the mind is a powerful aid to spiritual matters of *prayer, *study, *meditation, and so on. Thus the mind should be valued for its roles in *spiritual formation, complementing the holistic nature of people who are created in the image of God.

miracle. An extraordinary, divine occurrence that goes beyond natural explanation. Some people define a miracle as that which breaks the laws of nature, while other definitions consider God to work extraordinarily through nature, or both. With regard to the prevalence of miracles, some Christians believe that miracles occur daily, but that we are too faithless or oblivious to recognize and appreciate them. Other Christians believe that miracles are uncommon, even in *Scripture, and that we ought not to feel entitled to their occurrence, though we should not lose heart in praying for them. Certainly how one defines a miracle significantly affects how one prays (or does not pray) for miracles to occur. Spiritually, Christians throughout church history have been powerfully encouraged and emboldened in their spiritual lives and ministries due to the occurrence of miracles. Certainly Jesus considered the miracles performed during his ministry as verifications of his being the Messiah (or Christ) and of the authority and truth of his teachings (e.g., Matthew 11:2-6; Mark 2:3-12). Finally, Jesus gave his *disciples authority to perform miracles in the future, both during the time of the first-century church and for the future (e.g., Matthew 10:1).

miracles, working of, gift of. A special enabling of the Holy *Spirit that empowers believers to perform the miraculous. The gift of working miracles is variously understood as empowerment to perform miracles, or to serve as the instrument through which miracles occur. Because of how Paul describes the gift of the "working of miracles" in 1 Corinthians 12:10, it is thought that the gifting may not be permanent but situational depending on God's ultimate purpose for the role miracles play in our lives.

monasticism. An *ascetic way of life that emphasizes withdrawal from the world in order to focus on loving and *imitating *Jesus Christ. Monasticism may be practiced by individuals in isolation (eremitic monasticism) or by a community that believes *spiritual disciplines are best pursued with the support and accountability of others (cenobitic monasticism). Monasticism was rooted in the NT's call for Christians not to participate in idolatry, resulting in their avoiding the common social practices, and thus society itself, which sometimes led to their persecution. In the fourth century, early monastics followed the practices of Antony in Egypt, and in the sixth century, Benedict formulated rules for monastic communities, under the authority of an abbot (or vicar). In the twelfth century, Bernard of Clairvaux renewed Benedictine spirituality in the Cistercian order, emphasizing strict observance of the *Rules of Benedict. In such communities, monks shaped their lives around vows taken for spiritual *purification, for example, vows of *poverty, *celibacy, and *obedience. Today they own nothing, marry no one, and obey God without restraint. Their way of life is structured not to impede these vows or their devotion to prayer. The work they do is simple, only enough to sustain their way of life. Farming and the transcribing of scriptural manuscripts were important occupations in this type of community during medieval times. Spiritually, monasticism was (and continues to be) important because, even if one cannot live as a monk, their way of life serves as a living analogy for Christian devotion to God and the caution Christians should observe toward society. Reformation Protestants rejected monasticism because they did not believe that Christians needed to live in a commune to be unencumbered by the world and to flourish spiritually in service to God and others.

monk. A man whose life is dedicated entirely to God, taking vows of *obedience, *poverty, and chastity, in order to join a monastic community. Originally, the word had to do with living alone (Gk., *monachos*, "single, solitary"), but over time monks joined various ascetic communities for the sake of growing spiritually and for serving others. Catholic, Orthodox, and Anglican monks start as novices, taking temporary vows before making permanent vows to remain in a monastery. They may become ordained priests, but not necessarily. The term refers only to men; women who take similar vows are called nuns.

mortify, mortification. The self-denial that Christians perform as acts of *praise, thanks, and *obedience to God. Since *salvation is a gift by *grace, for which Christians do nothing to work or merit, they are to mortify (or wound) *sin in humble submission and in response to the vivification of God's grace for sanctification. John Calvin described mortification as a believer's participation in the sanctification process through resisting *temptation to sin and replacing sinful *habits with spiritual habits, such as *prayer and *worship. In *ascetic church traditions, mortification may include extreme measures, such as self-*flagellation.

music. Instrumental or vocal sounds, used especially to enhance *worship, *singing, and other celebrative practices. Christian music regularly occurs communally in church-related services, and is thought to be spiritually celebrative, conducive for people in focusing on God, and receiving spiritual succor from God. In both the OT and NT, reference is made to the importance of music for worshiping God. Music enhances worship by involving multiple senses: sight, sound, feeling. The emotion music invokes is particularly important; it elevates the expression of worship from reason to heart. For example, music complements the singing of *psalms, *hymns, and spiritual *songs (Ephesians 5:19).

mystery. That which people do not immediately know or understand. *Scripture describes some mysteries as being revealed (e.g., Romans 16:5; Ephesians 3:3-9); other mysteries have to do with the ongoing work of an infinite God within finite people (e.g., 1 Corinthians 15:51; Ephesians 5:32; 1 Timothy 3:16). The apostle Paul described Christians as "stewards of God's mysteries"; they live "by faith, not by sight" (see 1 Corinthians 4:1; 2 Corinthians 5:7). Because God transcends human knowledge, people must rely on God's revelation about *salvation and about spiritual matters. Such revelation, for example, as found in Scripture, is sufficient for salvation and for *spiritual formation. Christian *mystics especially emphasize the mysteries associated with people's relationship with God.

mystic. An *ascetic follower of God, seeking intimate knowledge and *union (or communion) with God, using various means of self-denial, *meditation, and *contemplation. Mystic spirituality includes a wide range of spiritual *experiences, ranging from relaxation and daily routine, on the one hand, to mystical rapture and *ecstasy, on the other hand.

mysticism. A type of Christian spirituality that emphasizes an especially intimate relationship with God that is ineffable or mysterious, culminating in *union (or communion) with God. Sometimes Christian spirituality has been identified synonymously with the word *mysticism*. However, mysticism is thought to be the most esoteric form of Christian spirituality, sometimes claiming secret knowledge. Origen was an early mystic and systematizer of mystical beliefs in the third century, considering allegorical interpretations of *Scripture to be the most revelatory about our relationship with God. In the sixth century, Pseudo-Dionysius emphasized three stages of mysticism: *purification (purgative way), *meditation (illuminative way), and union with God (*unitive way). Other notable mystics in church history include Meister Eckhart (thirteenth century), Catherine of Siena (fourteenth century), Discalced *Carmelites (sixteenth century), and French *quietists (seventeenth century). Some Christians in church history have considered mysticism too mysterious, fearing that participants may lose their sense of self (and reasoning) into the divine, reminiscent of *gnostic or occult phenomena in other religions. Christians have never had consensus regarding mysticism. For example, Martin Luther lauded the medieval book titled *Theologia Germanica*, which contained a mystical path of perfection, but John Calvin considered its mysticism to be spiritually poisonous.

N

naming and claiming. The belief that promises in *Scripture are directed to all Christians and need to be claimed in faith. Sometimes "naming and claiming" is also known as "promise claiming," which is related to word of faith and prosperity theology.

new birth. An analogy for *conversion that brings the promise of *eternal life and the spiritual growth God brings to believers (1 Peter 1:3). It is as if people are born anew (John 3:3), and spiritual regeneration begins as God's *Spirit works to renew believers in the *image of God.

new self. A reference to how believers are to "clothe" themselves in righteousness and *holiness, allowing God to transform them spiritually (Ephesians 4:24; Colossians 3:10). Although believers may not immediately experience transformation, it is expected that God's *Spirit works in their lives in order to mold them into greater *Christlikeness, restoring the *image of God in which they were created. *Scripture contrasts the new self with the "old self" (Ephesians 4:22; Colossians 3:9).

Nicene Creed. The statement of Christian beliefs formulated at the first and second ecumenical church councils, in 325 and 381 respectively. The creed was developed in the ancient church to combat a variety of heresies about the person and work of *Jesus Christ. It is still recited in the Roman Catholic *Mass, Orthodox Divine Liturgy, and Anglican rites for Holy

*Communion. Throughout church history, Christians have found the public and private recitation of the Nicene Creed—the earliest ecumenical statement of Christian beliefs—to be a fortification of their spiritual as well as theological well-being.

numerology. Study of the symbolic meaning of numbers, especially for the sake of determining religious meaning. Certain numbers have been important to Christians and to their spirituality. In Scripture, the numbers seven, twelve, and forty occur numerous times in both the OT and NT and are thus considered significant, spiritually as well as theologically. In church *tradition, certain numbers occur frequently, for example, the number three, alluding especially to beliefs and practices related to the doctrine of the *Trinity. Nevertheless, Christians have generally rejected the mystical or supernatural meaning of numbers, especially the pursuit of hidden meaning in numbers. Numbers are important more for reasons of tradition or for mnemonic reasons than for anything else.

O

obedience. Compliance with *laws, precepts, and *teachings, especially of those found in *Scripture. In the OT, God gave commandments and holiness codes to obey, the most famous being the Ten Commandments (Exodus 20:1-17). *Covenantal relationships that God established with the Israelites were conditioned on obedience to God's commandments. In the NT, *Jesus Christ affirmed OT "law" and "prophets" (Matthew 5:17), and commanded his disciples to "to obey everything that I have commanded you" (Matthew 28:20). Nevertheless, people are not saved by their obedience, good works, or merit. They are saved "by grace . . . through faith"; however, *grace and *faith are expected to produce "good works" (Ephesians 2:8-10). The commensurability of faith and good works is a theme emphasized in the book of James (esp. James 2:14-26). Spiritually, obedience to the *teachings of Scripture has been considered essential to Christian understanding and living. In addition, obedience to church leadership and teachings has been considered wise and fruitful for spiritual well-being and formation.

Offices. *See* Hours.

oil, anointing with. The practice of putting oil on the head of
sick people as others pray for them. This might be done, for example, by the elders of a church. Often oil is applied in the sign
of the *cross on a person's forehead. Anointing is most often
used for praying over the sick (e.g., James 5:14). In some Christian traditions the anointing of oil also is used for prayers on
special occasions, such as *intercession, ordaining ministers, or
when giving a prophetic word. In the Roman Catholic Church,
anointing of the sick is one of seven *sacraments, especially
for those whose sickness endangers their life. In the Orthodox
Church, this sacrament is called holy unction and is offered at
various *liturgies during the church year.

open theology (or open theism). The belief that God chooses not
to know the future, or that some or all of the future is unknow-
able, even to God. As such, the future is not determined, and
*prayer becomes especially meaningful in petitioning God for
help. Because the future and God's knowledge of it is "open,"
prayer may change God's mind (e.g., Exodus 32:14; Amos 7:2-6).

ordination. The consecration of a person to the priesthood or
ministry in various Christian churches. Ordination is considered a high spiritual vocation, to which individuals are called
by God, and confirmed through the corporate discernment of
churches. Also called holy orders in the Catholic, Orthodox, and
Anglican traditions, ordination is considered a *sacrament. In
Protestantism, all believers are thought to be ministers—"holy
priesthood" (1 Peter 2:5). Be that as it may, most Protestants believe that God calls individuals to the vocation or office of priest
(minister, pastor), and thus are ordained, thereafter giving leadership to the spiritual care and ministries of churches.

Our Father. The first words to the *Lord's Prayer, which is how
Jesus taught his disciples to pray. It may be used as another
name for the Lord's Prayer (also Lat., *Pater Noster*). Catholics
may be asked by a priest to pray the Our Father as an act of
*penance for the *sacrament of reconciliation.

Oxford movement. A British renewal movement in the nineteenth
century, which advocated that Protestants return to Catholic beliefs, values, and practices. Correspondingly, members of the

Oxford movement thought that the return to Catholic spiritual practices would best help Christians.

P

passion. A reference to "suffering" (Lat., *passio*), which may serve spiritual purposes. Most often the word has been used by Christians to talk about the passion of *Jesus Christ, who suffered humiliation and crucifixion for our *salvation. However, *passion* (or *passions*) may also refer to the vice of inordinate human desires and lusts, which thwart Christian virtue and Christlike living.

patience. The quality of being tolerant and long-suffering, which is spiritually beneficial. *Scripture describes patience as a result of God's Holy *Spirit at work in the lives of believers, and as such is a sign of spiritual maturity. Patience is evidence of the *fruit of the Spirit in a believer's life (Galatians 5:22).

peace. Rest and tranquility, especially of one's spiritual well-being. *Jesus promised peace that surpasses human understanding for those who believe in him for *salvation (e.g., Philippians 4:7). Christians ritualistically "pass the peace" in some church services, emulating the words of Jesus when he first appeared to the *disciples after his resurrection, when they were fearful (e.g., John 20:19-21). The Christian understanding of peace continues and expands on the Hebrew understanding of peace: *shalom. Growth in spirituality includes growth in peace, with regard to the present as well as future life.

Pelagianism. A historic heresy, representing the sufficiency of natural human *freedom for meriting *salvation and for producing spiritual growth. In the fifth century, *Augustine accused Pelagius of advocating salvation by works, emphasizing human rather than divine initiation, for people's salvation and spiritual growth. Semi-Pelagianism is a variation of Pelagianism, which puts greater emphasis on the role of God's gracious involvement in our lives, but still requires human initiation for both salvation and *spiritual formation.

penance. Words or deeds of reparation for past *sins or failings, done for the sake of spiritual and relational restoration. Penance is a biblical principle, modeled in penitents like Zacchaeus, who made monetary reparations for those he had unjustly treated (Luke 19:1-10). Historically, Catholics have made reparations an important part of the sacrament of reconciliation (previously known as *confession). In doing penance, penitents may be directed by confessor priests to say prayers of reparation, or to make right injustices that have been done.

penitence. A repentant, contrite spirit important for spiritual well-being. Penitence is important for spiritual *humility and reception of God's *grace. Penitents are those who *repent to God or others, sometimes making reparations for their wrongdoing.

Pentecost. The day the Holy *Spirit came fully to work in and through Christians. In Acts 2:1-31, the Holy Spirit dramatically came on about 120 followers of Jesus Christ; they spoke in *tongues (other languages) and were empowered to minister. Some Christians consider Pentecost to represent the birthday of the *church, and it is celebrated as a *holy day among Catholic, Orthodox, and Protestant churches. Pentecostals do not think that Pentecost represents a single historical event, but is paradigmatic of how all Christians should be baptized with the Holy Spirit, in the same way it happened on Pentecost.

Pentecostal spirituality (or Charismatic spirituality). A type of spirituality that emphasizes the *gifts of the Holy Spirit, which empowers Christians for ministry as well as for spiritual formation. *Tongues speaking is often considered the tangible evidence of *baptism with the Holy Spirit and spiritual fullness. Knowledge of and use of spiritual gifts, especially speaking in tongues, is considered a heightened expression of spirituality, which all Christians should desire.

Pentecostalism. A movement that affirms the spiritual importance of Holy Spirit baptism and *gifts of the Spirit. In particular, Pentecostals affirm *baptism with the Holy Spirit as a subsequent and distinct event after *conversion, at which time the Holy *Spirit gives the believer spiritual gifts for *edification of the *church. In classic Pentecostalism, speaking in tongues is considered the physical evidence of Holy Spirit baptism. Pentecostalism came to prominence in the twentieth century, most notably at the Azusa Street Revival. Pentecostal churches often began because Pentecostal believers were kicked out of existing churches and denominations. Be that as it may, the Pentecostal movement has influenced almost every church and denomination, refocusing Christian understandings about the person and work of the Holy Spirit in people's spiritual lives.

perfect, perfection. The goal, or end, which primarily applies to the spiritual and moral preeminence of God. Christians are called to be perfect, which involves *Christlikeness and the perfecting of love; it is the culmination of God's sanctifying *grace and people's total spiritual consecration. In the Sermon on the Mount, Jesus said, "Be perfect, therefore, as your heavenly Father is perfect" (Matthew 5:48). In 1 Thessalonians 5:23, the apostle Paul says, "May the God of peace himself sanctify you entirely." Although the prospect of becoming perfect seems daunting, it is little wonder that God, who is perfect, would lead Christians to any goal other than spiritual, physical, and social perfection. In church history, perfection has been a repeated goal for *spiritual formation. For example, Orthodox Christians sought *theosis (Gk., "deification"), and Catholic Christians followed counsels of perfection (*see* perfection, counsels of). Among Protestants, John Wesley thought that believers could achieve Christlike *love in this life, which he described as Christian perfection, or entire *sanctification.

perfection, counsels of. Catholic practices by which a Christian is able to become spiritually perfect (or complete, mature, holy). Certain scriptural precepts are considered essential for *salvation, but other *teachings of *Scripture and the *church aid one in becoming more *Christlike, more *perfect. Three counsels of perfection include chastity, *poverty, and *obedience; these have not been viewed by the church as necessary vows for salvation but are acts that go above the ordinary requirements of Christians. Monastic orders keep additional counsels of perfection, whether or not they are named as such. The counsels include *ascetic practices that are intended to free the *soul to *worship God more fully by removing obstacles for spiritual growth. Reformation Protestants rejected counsels of perfection, arguing that scriptural and church teachings are for all Christians.

perseverance of the saints. The belief that those who have been *justified and saved by *faith in *Jesus Christ will ultimately persist as believers until the end of their earthly lives. Those who hold to this view believe that those whom God elects to be saved will persevere by God's sovereign hand. This phrase is often used synonymously with eternal security, but some make a distinction between the two. They argue that eternal security implies that one's actions after salvation do not matter; one may go on willfully sinning and still be assured salvation. Perseverance of the saints, on the other hand, states that those who are saved ought not to go on willfully sinning. *See also* assurance of salvation.

petition. A request to God for one's needs for comfort, *encouragement, guidance, and empowerment, as well as for the overcoming of undesirable circumstances and crises that arise. For many people, petition is their primary understanding of prayer. It may include intercessory petitions for others. Petition is a significant part of prayer, and *Scripture exhorts it as something desired by God, not something inherently self-centered (e.g., Ezra 8:23; Psalm 20:5). God wants people to make their petitions known, though people ought not to think that they are entitled to having God answer every prayer (e.g., Daniel 3:17-18; Matthew 26:39). On the contrary, God may not always answer prayers as petitioned, since God has people's greater well-being in mind, individually and socially. People in Scripture make petitionary prayers for help in times of trouble, deliverance from enemies, guidance, healing, mercy, and grace. Hannah, for example, makes a very specific request for the birth of a child (e.g., 1 Samuel 2). No petition should be thought of as being too small for God's consideration, and people ought to be encouraged to bring all their requests to God.

Pietism. The Christian revitalization movement in seventeenth-century continental Europe, associated with Philipp Jakob Spener, who acknowledged the felt dimension of spirituality and *spiritual formation that Christians may experience by *grace through *faith. Spener emphasized that it was the privilege of Christians to experience vitality in their growth in piety (or *Christlikeness), especially as they met in small accountability groups. In his "schools of piety" (Lat., *collegia pietatis*) Spener emphasized the importance of Christian community for spiritual growth, along with the study of *Scripture and other *devotional literature. The *experiential dimension especially inspired believers, who thought that continental Protestantism had become too intellectual and ceremonial. Subsequently, Pietism had a great deal of influence, spiritually vitalizing Moravians, Methodists, and other Christian traditions.

pilgrimage. A trip undertaken for spiritual purposes. People travel to special or holy locations for spiritual encouragement. Silvia of Egeria is the earliest known pilgrim to the Holy Land, in the fourth century. Catholics yearly travel to holy sites around the world, seeking to pray and grow as Christians (e.g., Santiago de Compostela, Spain, and Lourdes, France). Protestants also undertake informal pilgrimages, for example, to Israel as well as to the sites of prominent church leaders or centers of ministry. Some describe symbolically the Christian life as a pilgrimage, and evaluate the ups and downs of their progress as a kind of spiritual journey. For example, John Bunyan's *Pilgrim's Progress* is an allegory in journey form about *conversion, spiritual growth through various trials and *temptations, and finally the attainment of a heavenly destination.

poetry. A form of literature that uses aesthetics, rhythm, and meter, especially for the sake of spiritual well-being. The OT includes a great deal of poetry, particularly in its wisdom literature (e.g., *Psalms). Poetry can be stimulating for the sake of comforting and encouraging growth in one's relationship with God. *Meditation on biblical poems (or any spiritual poems) can be especially helpful in *spiritual formation. Poetry can be read, spoken, sung, and chanted, and is frequently found in public *worship and *liturgy for the sake of aiding people's spiritual awareness.

popcorn prayer. An unstructured order of group prayer, in which one person is assigned to open and another to close, and then others pray in between as they feel led. Prayers may be as short as one sentence, or they may be longer.

poverty. Impoverishment in its many forms, spiritual as well as physical and economic. *Scripture repeatedly emphasizes the need to care for the poor in their many needs (e.g., Matthew 25:31-46). In some biblical passages, poverty is considered a *blessing (e.g., Luke 6:20). Although Scripture talks about ways to avoid impoverishment (e.g., Proverbs 20:13), Christians are to care for the poor, regardless of why they are poor. Such care should involve compassion for the symptoms and also advocacy on behalf of the causes of poverty. Some Christians have followed *ascetic practices of self-imposed poverty (frugality, self-*sacrifice) for the sake of focusing more on spiritual growth. *Jesus modeled frugal, simple living, which inspired later Christ followers for their own living. *Monastic practices and vows of poverty, for example, by Catholic monks, reinforced the spiritual virtuosity of self-imposed poverty for the sake of better loving and serving God and others. *See also* mendicant spirituality.

practice of the presence of God. The affirmation that spiritual concerns related to God and God's presence may be recollected and practiced anytime and anywhere, no matter how menial or mundane our life and work may be. The seventeenth-century *Carmelite known as Brother Lawrence emphasized how people may practice the presence of God in the midst of commonplace working, for example, while cooking in a kitchen or farming. No time is too mundane or secular to serve as an occasion for spiritual intimacy with God and for growth as a Christian.

praise. The expression of *adoration, acclamation, and *celebration, especially to God, who is supremely worthy of honor. Praise represents a prominent form of *prayer, when God is honored for who he is and what he does for people. Scripture exhorts people to praise God, as well as to thank God, for deliverance, empowerment, material aid, and help in trouble (e.g., Psalm 66:1-20; Philippians 4:6). Praise may be a response, either to an action of God that affects the person giving praise or to a revelation of God's character. Praise can either be private or public. It can come from the intellect or from the emotions; praise can occur in response to a spiritual encounter with God, which transcends (but does not exclude) the physical and emotional. Praise, in effect, glorifies God. However, it also positively influences those praising God, by giving people a proper perspective on their relationship to God and others.

pray, prayer. Talking with God, talking to God, and listening to God. People reverently and devoutly entreat God in prayer (Lat., *oratio*). Prayer is thought to be the most immediate, most common, and most intimate way to approach God, communicate with God, or to grow in relationship with God. In the OT, it is God's will that people should pray, asking God for help; and God blesses those who pray (e.g., Psalm 4:1; 141:2). In the NT, *Jesus Christ prayed often, taught his *disciples to pray, and encouraged them to persevere in prayer (e.g., Luke 6:12; 18:1; Ephesians 6:18).

Prayer occurs many ways: spoken and unspoken, private and public, individual and corporate, spontaneous and prepared, *thanksgiving and *petition, *praise and *lament, bold and humble, *mystical and *liturgical, in *tongues and in interpretation of tongues.

Prayer is discussed extensively in *Scripture. Jesus' advice to his disciples in teaching them to pray became known as the *Lord's Prayer (Matthew 6:9-13; Luke 11:1-4), which became a classic model for prayer that Christians have emulated throughout church history. Scripture offers promises to those who pray, and encourages persistence in prayer (e.g., Luke 18:1-8). Numerous answers to prayer are listed, but God does not always answer as people pray, since God's will transcends human will. Scripture also gives advice for effective prayer, and how to avoid ineffective prayer (e.g., Matthew 21:22).

In church history, Christians have differed with regard to what prayer accomplishes. Some emphasize that, because God is sovereign in ordaining all that happens, prayer does not change God and instead changes the person who prays. Other Christians emphasize that God foreknows how people will pray, since God graciously gives them *freedom to petition him; then God may change their circumstances, given God's comprehensive knowledge of what is best for those who pray. Those who pray are never entitled to receive everything (or anything) for which they ask, since God alone knows what is best for them.

pray and work (Lat., *ora et labora*). The combination of prayer and work emphasized by the *Rule of Benedict to balance spirituality and physical labor in *monastic Christian living. The phrase has been used by other Christians in balancing spiritual and work-related priorities.

prayer, affirmative. An approach to prayer that focuses on positive outcomes rather than on negative circumstances and on spiritual strengths rather than weaknesses. Some consider this approach unduly influenced by positive thinking rather than biblical principles.

prayer alerts. Means by which prayer requests are made known to groups of people. Nowadays phone or text messages are sent out en masse. In addition, various social media are used to send out prayer requests.

prayer as thanksgiving. *See* thanksgiving.

prayer, asking. *See* petition.

prayer at mealtime. Prayer before eating a meal. It may include *blessing the food and the preparers, *thanksgiving for God's provision, and any other prayer needs. *Jesus notably prayed before his last supper with the *disciples (e.g., Matthew 26:26). *Puritan Christians were known for their *habit of praying (or saying grace) before meals.

prayer bench. A bench or altar made to assist one in kneeling prayer, usually located in the front of a church. Some churches provide benches in pews, known as kneelers, for aiding prayer in worship services. In the nineteenth century, Charles Finney talked about an "anxious bench," where people could come to pray for spiritual guidance and strength or to convert to Christianity.

prayer chain. A list of people committed to praying for needs as they arise, for example, in churches. When the initiators of the prayer chain receive a request for prayer, they contact other people—individually or collectively—on the chain and tell them the request. They then pray and contact other people on the prayer chain. Prayer chains may occur face-to-face, or by phone, email, and other social media.

prayer closet. A secluded place used for prayer away from others, based on Jesus' directions for prayer in Matthew 6:8. Common adaptations include a prayer chair or any place specifically set aside for prayer in *solitude.

prayer education. Teaching others to pray. Jesus Christ famously taught his disciples to pray, using words that later became known as the *Lord's Prayer (Matthew 6:9-13). Teaching people to pray may occur individually or collectively, informally or formally, teaching different types and ways to pray. It is believed that educating people to pray will help them become better prepared in their attitudes and spirit as well as in becoming more practiced in different types of prayer.

prayer, extemporaneous. Spontaneous prayer that is not scripted liturgically or formed on a model or set time. It may occur privately or publicly in a worship service. The content of extemporaneous prayer can involve any topic, and some consider it a more personal and heartfelt way to pray.

prayer for healing. A *petitionary prayer asking God specifically for healing. In James 5:13-16, believers are instructed to pray for those who are sick, anointing them with *oil. Prayer for healing may include miraculous, instantaneous healing, but it may also include prayers for hastened recoveries from injury, emotionally as well as physically. Even though many prayers for healing do not result in supernatural intervention, despite participants who are full of faith and fervency, the Christian church still emphasizes the importance of praying for those who are sick or injured.

prayer for the dead. A prayer offered on behalf of those who have died, perhaps for their *salvation or to aid them in the afterlife. In the early church, Christians prayed for those who died, and later Catholic and Orthodox Christians prayed particularly for those experiencing spiritual *purification in *purgatory, before entering heaven. Protestants generally have not believed that prayer for the dead is necessary, though not prohibited.

prayer language, private. The belief that, in addition to public prayer in *tongues, Christians pray in tongues privately as well (1 Corinthians 14:4, 28). Paul seems to talk about this kind of prayer as *devotional in nature, rather than for the *edification of others. Historically, *Pentecostals who emphasize speaking in tongues have emphasized both private and public prayer languages.

prayer list. Lists used as aids to prayer. They may include lists of people for whom to pray, topics used for long-term prayer, and short-term lists of immediate concern. Prayers lists may be used on a daily basis, weekly basis, or in some other fashion.

prayer meeting. Any group gathering for the sake of prayer, usually in churches during midweek. In Acts 12:5-17, Christians met in the house of Mary the mother of John in order to pray for the apostle Peter, who had been imprisoned. Prayer meetings may be extemporaneous or regularly scheduled.

prayer of aspiration. A short prayer crying out to God or to *Jesus Christ. A prayer of aspiration may be as short as saying the name "Jesus!" Other prayers may include, "Jesus, help me," or "Thank you, God." Sometimes Catholics refer to these aspirations as ejaculatory prayers.

prayer of blessing. A prayer of intercession typically performed in the presence of those for whom a *blessing is prayed. A well-known prayer of blessing is the *benediction given at the end of worship services. Prayers of blessing are often given by clergy for their congregation, parents for their children, and during significant occasions (e.g., *marriages, *ordinations, sending of missionaries).

prayer of forgiveness. Prayer that asks for God to forgive sin, following the example of the petition in the *Lord's Prayer— "forgive us our debts, as we forgive our debtors" (Matthew 6:12). Prayers of forgiveness may occur at the time of *conversion. Although God does not hold the guilt of *sin against Christians, due to the atonement of Jesus Christ, God still expects them to pray with ongoing *penitence for sin and to repent of sins they commit. Prayers for forgiveness may occur individually or collectively. Some churches publicly pray weekly *confessions for sin, acknowledging God's forgiveness of them.

prayer of silence. The practice of seeking to commune wordlessly with God. It resembles *listening prayer.

prayer partners. The practice of having a group of two or more people who commit to praying for and with each other regularly. Prayer partners may meet face-to-face, or they may pray for one another from long distances. People may become prayer partners for short periods of time or for many years.

prayer positions (or postures). Praying in different physical positions with the intent of allowing physical posture to enhance one's prayers. Consider the following examples. First, kneeling prayer can be done with a prayer bench located at the back of pews, called kneelers, or directly on the ground. Kneeling is a sign of respect, and such prayers are especially intended to honor God and make supplication before God. Second, some people find it helpful to sit in a chair for extended times of prayer. The stability of a chair allows them to focus their minds and thoughts on God. Third, some stand during their prayer times as a sign of honor to God. Orthodox Christians stand through most of their public worship services as a sign of respect, reverence, and submission to God. Others find that standing with other people, perhaps in a circle and even holding hands, is conducive for prayer. Fourth, prayer standing with arms outstretched helps some people experience a heightened sense of praise and worship of God, freeing one's sense of spirituality.

prayer, remembering. The practice of remembering a past event in one's life and prayerfully meditating on it in dialogue with God. One generally focuses on events where one knew God's presence in a deep way, or that were particularly joyful or painful, as one seeks to relate them to present life. Remembering prayer may help in the healing of memories.

prayer, repetitive. The repetition of generally short, formulaic prayers. For example, *hesychasm has advocated repetitive use of the *Jesus Prayer, for the sake of promoting introspection, tranquility, and *silence.

prayer request. An entreaty or wish for intercessory prayer for oneself or for others. In *Scripture, prayer requests are made among fellow believers (e.g., 1 Thessalonians 5:25; 2 Thessalonians 3:1), and that practice continues today. Prayer requests also happen in churches, wherein attendees are asked to speak or write down their desires for prayer so that others may pray for them. Variations include having a web form to fill out or a designated phone number to call or text.

prayer room. A room where people can go for prayer, especially before or after worship services in churches. Church members are often available to pray for those who want to make their requests known.

prayer, sensual. Engaging the physical senses in aiding prayer. Sensual prayer may include the sounds of *music and *singing, the sights of artistry and architecture, and the smells of incense; or it may also include sounds, sights, and smells of nature.

prayer, singing. A prayer that is sung. It may be sung audibly or silently, individually or collectively, liturgically or extemporaneously. Some *experience the singing of prayers as helpful in communicating with God, letting the lyrics of Christian songs aid in their *worship.

prayer time. A time specifically designated for prayer. Such times may be individual or corporate, informal or formal. *Scripture encourages people to take time to pray, and scheduled times may enhance the value of one's prayer life. In church history, liturgical *Hours are set aside throughout the day for prayer. Korean Christians promote *sae byuk kido* (Kor., "early morning prayer"), which emphasizes the importance of starting every day in prayer.

prayer, twenty-four-hour. Prayer by a group or an individual lasting nonstop for twenty-four hours. For example, churches may use a sign-up sheet to assign different people time slots to pray throughout the day and night. This type of prayer is done for special events or while approaching major decisions. Around-the-clock prayer can be done for any length of time, and not just for twenty-four hours (e.g., 24/7 prayer).

prayer, unanswered. Petitionary prayer that is not thought to be answered by God. Christians differ with regard to whether God does or does not answer all prayers. Certainly *Scripture says that God hears all our prayers (e.g., Psalm 65:2; 66:19-20). Some Christians argue that God does not answer all prayers and that people ought not to feel entitled to have all prayers answered, since God may have other plans for the one who prayed, or for the prayer prayed. Others argue that God answers all prayers, though some prayers may not be answered immediately, or they may be answered differently than prayed. The difference may be nominal; however, those who believe that God does not answer every prayer also believe that such occasions may serve as opportunities for individuals to grow spiritually.

prayer, vocal. Praying out loud that emphasizes liturgical and spoken dialogue with God, including prescribed prayers of *praise, *thanksgiving, *petition, and *intercession. Catholics refer to vocal prayer in contrast to *mental prayer, which is more dialogical, *meditative, and *contemplative.

prayer walk. Praying while one walks around a community or prescribed area. This can be done individually or as part of a group. Common topics of such prayer are *thanksgiving for ways one knows God has worked in that place and *intercessions for the people who are geographically near.

prayer, welcoming. A *contemplative practice that welcomes physical and emotional discomfort, lets go of the desire to control the situation or cause of the discomfort, and concludes by welcoming God's presence into the situation. The welcoming prayer stems from the belief that God is in all things and can bring good out of them. Therefore, welcoming prayer requires reorientation so that a negative situation can be viewed as beneficial.

prayer without ceasing. *See* constant prayer.

praying in tongues. Prayer that occurs in *tongues. Typically, praying in tongues refers to the spiritual *gift of a personal or heavenly language, known only to the speaker and God. However, in the book of Acts, some instances of speaking in tongues may have been languages in the ancient Near East. According to 1 Corinthians 14:4, Paul states that speaking in tongues edifies the individual. Speaking in tongues is also edifying for the church when it is interpreted. *See also* tongues, gift of; tongues, speaking in.

praying the alphabet. Praying through the alphabet, thinking of something to pray about for each letter of the alphabet, in order to expand on the breadth and depth of ways one may pray.

praying the Bible. *See* lectio divina.

praying the Hours. *See* Hours.

preaching. The public proclamation of biblical and Christian beliefs, values, and practices, usually in public worship services, such as in churches. *Jesus Christ commanded his followers to proclaim the *gospel in both word and deed (e.g., Acts 10:34-43). Preaching was considered one of the marks of a true church by Protestants during the Reformation, but all church traditions preach sermons (also known as homilies). Sometimes preaching is thought of as a prophetic act. Spiritually, preaching represents one of the most common ways people receive biblical and Christian instruction for their formation in faith, hope, and love (*see* virtues, theological).

predestination. God's providential decrees with regard to the lives of people, especially for their *salvation and spiritual development. Although God's decrees are thought to be sovereign, most Christians believe that people are to respond voluntarily to these divine initiatives. The need for responsible decision making on the part of Christians is especially important for the sake of their spiritual growth. However, Christians differ with regard to the degree to which they believe that God predestines (or predetermines) people's lives and salvation. Those who believe in specific (or meticulous) sovereignty argue that God effectually (or irresistibly) determines the events of people's lives, for example, including their election (regarding salvation) and reprobation (regarding damnation). Examples of specific sovereignty include Augustine, Martin Luther, John Calvin, and Karl Barth. On the other hand, those who believe in general sovereignty argue that God voluntarily gives people sufficient *freedom to accept or reject God's plans for their lives. Examples of general sovereignty include Thomas Aquinas, Thomas Cranmer, Jakob Arminius, and John Wesley. Consequently, those who place more emphasis on God's predestination emphasize God's control of their salvation and spiritual growth, whereas those who place more emphasis on God synergistically partnering with people emphasize God's expectation of responsible decision making with regard to their salvation and spiritual growth.

prophecy. Proclamation of God's words or message, especially with regard to *salvation and spiritual development. Prophecy may include communication about how God wants people to live here and now, involving a kind of forth-telling of God's words; it also may include communication about how God will relate with people in the future, involving a kind of foretelling of coming events. Prophetic utterances relate to people's spirituality and *spiritual formation as well as to other aspects of

God's will. The OT has a rich history of both forms of prophecy. God's forth-telling often had to do with how Israelites ought to live righteously, justly, and compassionately toward the poor, marginalized, and oppressed (*see* justice; liberation). God also foretold of future events, including prophecies about the Messiah. In the NT, prophecy is sometimes talked about as one of the *gifts of the Holy Spirit. Generally, prophecy promotes Christian living that emphasizes compassion as well as advocacy on behalf of those who are poor, marginalized, and oppressed. Prophetic utterances in *Scripture addressed physical, social, political, and economic issues as well as spiritual ones. Thus prophets and their prophecies had holistic implications for those to whom the prophecies were given. Some consider prophetic advocacy essential to social *activist understandings of Christian spirituality.

prophecy, gift of. A special enabling of the Holy *Spirit that empowers believers to speak on behalf of God. Prophecy is the most commonly listed gift of the Holy Spirit (Romans 12:6; 1 Corinthians 12:10, 29; Ephesians 4:11). It is considered especially important for proclamation and preaching of the *gospel. Paul thought prophecy valuable for building up the *church, whereas other gifts, for example, speaking in *tongues, were less valuable.

prophetic prayer. Prayer for or prayer declaring God's words for people, both for present and future circumstances. Prophetic prayers for the present often have to do with matters of *justice and counteracting marginalization and oppression in the world, and prophetic prayers for the future have to do with how Christians ought to live, individually and socially, in anticipation of the consummation of God's reign in the future.

prosperity theology. Belief that God intends for all Christians to experience blessings, both financial and physical (especially health) as well as spiritual. Hence, prosperity theology is sometimes known as the gospel of health and wealth, or as success theology. These blessings are attained through faith (e.g., *naming and claiming) and financial generosity (e.g., charity and church donations). Although Christians historically have acknowledged an interconnectedness between spiritual and physical dimensions, in *Scripture as well as in life, they have not equated spirituality with health and wealth.

prostrate prayer. Praying while lying face down on the ground, which communicates the *humility of the prayer as well as honor to God. Prostration in *Scripture is a sign of great earnestness (e.g., Matthew 2:11), and the practice continued throughout church history. Today, Christians may prostrate themselves in prayer to heighten their spiritual urgency in encounter with God.

providence. *See* predestination.

prudence. *See* wisdom.

psalm/psalms. Spiritual poems or *songs, written primarily for the sake of praising God, and which also contain rich theological and spiritual meaning. Hebrew people recited or sang psalms in public *worship, with and without instrumentation, though they are equally meaningful for use by individuals. The book of Psalms contains the largest, best-known compilation of psalms in *Scripture. For the sake of spiritual consolation and growth, few books of Scripture are read more than the book of Psalms.

Psalms, book of. A book in the OT that contains 150 psalms. Tradition attributes the Psalms to David king of Israel, but the book itself mentions other authors such as Asaph (Psalms 50; 73–83), and biblical scholars think that the psalms may have been compiled over several centuries. The book of Psalms has long been used by Jews as well as Christians for public and personal *worship of God. No other book is used as extensively in spiritually comforting, *encouraging, and guiding readers for their formation in holy living. Readers consider the book to touch on the deepest emotions people have, the struggles they *experience, and their longing for God.

purgatory. An intermediate place of purification to which, Catholics believe, Christians go after death if they failed in life to live righteously in obedience to *Scripture and the teachings of the church. Purgatory does not represent a second chance for *salvation. Rather, it requires the kind of purgative cleansing from sin about which Christians now ought to be involved. In contrast, most Protestant Christians reject the reality of purgatory, instead emphasizing the urgency for pursuing godly, holy living in this life.

purification (and purgation). The cleansing of *sin or the removal of earthly distractions that prevent one from relating with God and living godly lives. Christians in the early church believed that spiritual purification occurs as the result of the interaction between spiritual disciplines (e.g., *prayer, *meditation, *worship) and the Holy *Spirit's assistance. Some Protestant traditions believe that purification can only be accomplished by the Holy Spirit, through vivification and *mortification; other Protestant traditions believe that sanctifying *grace is given for the perfecting of love and holy living. In the Catholic tradition, purification also occurs in *purgatory for those who, in this life, failed to purge themselves spiritually and morally before entering heaven. In mysticism, purification represented the first of three stages of spiritual enlightenment: purification (purgative way), meditation (illuminative way), and *union with God (*unitive way).

Puritans. Reformed Christians who sought to purify the Church of England during the sixteenth and seventeenth centuries from the lingering theological and sacramental influence of Roman Catholicism. Puritans adopted moral rigor and austere lifestyles in their pursuit of *godliness, inspired by the theology and spiritual teachings of John Calvin. Puritans were influential in the early history of the United States, for example, through the theological and revivalist influence of Jonathan Edwards.

Q

questioning prayer. Asking questions of God from the perspective of *faith and an earnest desire to understand. In addition to the questions Job uplifted to God, *Jesus Christ asked questions, even while on the cross (Matthew 27:46). Questioning prayers can be asked about the future, current challenges, the meaning of life, the problem of *evil, and so on. The key is to be in dialogue with God through questions, which are asked for the sake of growing in one's faith, understanding, and relationship with God.

quietism. A type of spirituality that emphasizes *contemplation more than scriptural *meditation and vocal prayer (*see* prayer, vocal). During the seventeenth century, Catholic quietists such as Miguel de Molinos and Madame Guyon were condemned as heretics for emphasizing contemplation over meditation and for promoting union with and abandonment to God that super-seded historic Catholic beliefs. Among Protestants, branches of the Society of Friends (Quakers) have been known as quietists due to their silent waiting for God's *Spirit in unprogrammed worship services.

R

reading, spiritual. *See* lectio divina.

reason. The faculty by which people think logically, critically, and creatively, contributing to the spiritual well-being of people as well as other aspects of their lives. *Scripture repeatedly talks about the intellectual virtue of reasoning about God and about spiritual matters. In the King James Version of Scripture, Isaiah 1:18 says: "Come now, and let us reason together, saith the LORD." This emphasis on critical thinking and argumen-tative reasoning complements, rather than contradicts, biblical teachings and *spiritual formation. To be sure, Scripture warns people about how reason and knowledge may be misleading, and do not measure up to divine reason (1 Corinthians 1:18-31). Still, Christians need to be prepared to reason with unbeliev-ers, give apologetic reasons for the spiritual hope they have, and use reason to direct people toward God. Thus our faculty of reason aids people's holistic well-being and contributes to spiritual disciplines of prayer, study, meditation, and so on.

recitation. Repeating something aloud by memory, with signifi-cance for people's spiritual well-being. Christians have long emphasized the memorization of *Scripture as well as other spiritually informative *liturgy and literature. Repeating them out loud may benefit the individual reciting Scripture or other readings in addition to those who listen.

recollection. The faculty of remembering something, especially remembering those biblical verses and spiritual *teachings learned at a previous time (e.g., Deuteronomy 6:6-9). The spiritual practice of recollection is associated with the seventeenth-century *Carmelite monk named Brother Lawrence, who believed that we should *practice the presence of God no matter where we are or what we are doing. Even in the common business of working in a kitchen or farming, we may recollect, pray about, *meditate on, and *contemplate matters that benefit our spiritual formation.

reconciliation. One of several biblical terms used to describe *salvation, emphasizing how the atoning work of *Jesus Christ resulted in reconciling people with God. Reconciliation emphasizes the relational aspect of salvation. It occurs at the initiation of God (2 Corinthians 5:18-19), and results in peace with God, adoption as children, and access to God. Spiritually, reconciliation reinforces a relational understanding of Christian spirituality, and how the emphasis of spirituality has to do with the quality and intimacy of the loving relationship people have with God. The apostle Paul believed that reconciliation with God should also result in reconciliation with others, especially across racial, ethnic, and class lines.

redemption. One of the biblical terms to describe the atonement of *Jesus Christ, emphasizing the purchase or buying back of people's *salvation from *sin, death, and *Satan. Jesus is described as having redeemed us through his blood (Ephesians 1:7). In redeeming people, Jesus provided for their forgiveness of *sins, freedom from the law of judgment, and freedom to live a new life in Christ.

regeneration. God's work in renewing believers, including the restoration of people's righteousness and spirituality. It also has been called the *new birth or new creation. Regeneration is often paired theologically with *justification. It emphasizes the work of God's *Spirit in renewing the image of God in which people were created. Some Christians describe regeneration as initial *sanctification.

relaxation exercises. Physical, intellectual, and emotional practices used to calm oneself for *prayer, *meditation, and *contemplation of God. In particular, using means for physical relaxation (e.g., posture, breath control) help people focus on spiritual matters. Many prayer postures help people to relax before praying, and Christians sometimes borrow from yoga and other *ascetic practices, which benefit their health as well as their spiritual well-being.

relics. The physical remains of a *saint or venerated Christian, which Catholics and other Christians find spiritually encouraging in their *worship of God and *faith development. Relics are generally stored in church reliquaries.

repent, repentance. The regret and resolve people have as they turn away from *sin and turn to God in *faith. Repentance involves contrition for sin, *confession of it, and resolution no longer to sin. Scripture often talks about repentance as a condition for *salvation (e.g., Mark 1:15; Acts 2:38). Repentance is also considered a condition for the restorative dimensions of *sanctification. It helps to heal the effects of sin in one's life, aided by God's ongoing work of restoring the image of God in believers. Repentance does not end with conversion. There is a need for believers to repent of ongoing sin in their lives.

repentance after justification. *Confession and sorrow over *sin after conversion, which is needed for growth in holy living. Although people are saved by *grace through *faith, God expects them to repent of ongoing sin throughout their lives. Confession and *penance contribute to spiritual self-understanding and growth. John Wesley considered repentance after justification to be crucial for the purpose of becoming entirely sanctified (*see* sanctification, entire).

responsive reading. A worship practice involving the reading out loud of *Scripture by a leader, to which the people or congregation respond with their own reading of Scripture. Sometimes *liturgy is read responsively as well as Scripture in order to emphasize its importance for *worship and for *spiritual formation.

resurrection. The raising of believers in *Jesus Christ from the dead with new, heavenly bodies as well as the restoring of their personhood; what is more, resurrection has implications for believers' spiritual well-being here and now. Jesus was the "first fruits" of resurrection, when he reappeared bodily after his crucifixion and death (1 Corinthians 15:20). Jesus said that all will be resurrected, some to eternal reward and others to eternal punishment (e.g., Matthew 13:49-50). But their *eternal lives will be embodied as well as spiritual; they will not have only an ethereal existence. Resurrection should be distinguished from the resuscitation of people from death (e.g., Jairus's daughter, Lazarus), since the latter will die again. Resurrection is for eternity, and it represents the complete restoration of one's life, bodily and spiritually. In this life, the hope of resurrection serves as a stimulus for the spiritual formation of believers, recognizing that one's spiritual well-being is inextricably bound up with one's bodily well-being.

retreat (and advance). Withdrawal to a distant location for a short period of time for the sake of spiritual repose, *prayer, guidance, and practice of disciplines that aid one in *spiritual formation. Retreats may occur for a day, a weekend, or more. Korean Christians promote *kido won* (Kor., "prayer mountain"), emphasizing the importance of getting away to a mountainous (or some other kind of) retreat for the sake of prayer. Sometimes "retreats" are known as "advances," accentuating the spiritually advantageous aspect of the time away.

revival meeting. A worship event for the sake of evangelism and for renewing believers' spirituality and *holiness. Revival meetings may be held in churches or camps, of various sorts, and became popular in the United States during the First Great Awakening (eighteenth century) and Second Great Awakening (nineteenth century). For example, the Keswick movement promoted holiness in weeklong camp meetings. Emphasis was placed on making decisions during revival meetings, either to convert to Christianity or to rededicate one's life to holy, Christlike living.

rite. Usually the service for sacred events, including the wording used, for example, for *baptism and the *Lord's Supper. Certain words, phrases, and recitations have become powerful traditions in church services, which aid participants in the *worship of God as well as aid their spiritual well-being. For example, baptizing people "in the name of the Father and of the Son and of the Holy Spirit" is often considered an essential phrase for baptism (Matthew 28:19). Likewise, the recitation of Jesus' words for partaking in the Lord's Supper is needful for duly administering the *sacrament. Other words, phrases, and recitations—not specially associated with the sacraments—may also become essential for public worship services, such as the passing of the peace or saying amen. Rites are often associated with *rituals, and indeed the meaning of the two terms has been used synonymously.

ritual. Usually the practices for sacred events, especially those for the *sacraments, such as *baptism and *Lord's Supper. In the sacraments, rituals include the *water used in baptism, and the *bread and *wine in the Lord's Supper. Rituals may include a variety of devotional practices, for example, processions in public worship services, vestments, bowing, kneeling, incense, bells, and *footwashing. Such rituals aid people in their worship of God and in spiritual reflection and growth.

rosary. A form of prayer using a string of prayer beads—a rosary (Lat., *rosarium*, "crown of roses" or "garland of roses")—in order to keep track of a series of prayers, related primarily to *Jesus Christ and to *Mary, for the sake of *meditation and *contemplation. In praying the rosary, Christians recite sets of prayer, known as decades, which include the *Lord's Prayer, *Hail Mary, and *Glory Be. For centuries, Christians have found the rosary crucial in guiding their meditation and contemplation on all that God has provided for their *salvation through Jesus, and for their ongoing growth as Christians through the aid of the Holy *Spirit, Mary, and other *saints.

rule of life. A set of rules that governs a person's pattern or regimen of *spiritual disciplines, especially within the context of living with others in a monastic community. The *Rule of Benedict provides guidelines governing *Benedictine monasteries. However, there also are rules of life provided by Franciscans, *Ignatians, and others.

Rule of Benedict. The guidelines first devised by Benedict in the sixth century for *monastic life, led by an abbot (or vicar). Benedict's Rule was renewed and updated for monastic life under the leadership of Bernard of Clairvaux in the twelfth century. Basic precepts of these guidelines have been used for fifteen centuries by Catholics, since they are thought to hold a healthy balance in supporting individual spiritual needs and those of the monastic community.

S

sacrament. A sacred act in which Christians participate involving church-designated *rites and *rituals. In the early church, the word *sacramentum* (hallow, consecrate) was used to describe these sacred acts in Latin-speaking churches, and the word *mystērion* (mystery) was used in Greek-speaking churches. In Catholic churches, the sacraments have been thought to work *ex opere operato* (Lat., "from the work worked"); that is, the sacraments serve as an effective means or channel of God's grace for those who participate, when priests duly perform them; they are not just symbolic. There are seven Catholic sacraments: *baptism, *confirmation, *Eucharist, reconciliation, anointing of the sick (*see* oil, anointing with), holy matrimony (*see* marriage), and holy orders (*see* ordination). Orthodox churches also recognize these seven sacraments (some with slightly different names), and they are still often referred to as the Holy Mysteries. Regular participation in the sacraments ensures divine enablement for one's spiritual growth and healing as well as for *salvation. In contrast, Protestants believe that *faith represents the condition for the gracious efficacy of sacraments. In Protestant churches, the two sacraments practiced most often are baptism and the *Lord's Supper (or *Communion, *Eucharist,). For Martin Luther and John Calvin, the sacraments represented both a sign and seal of grace in the lives of faithful participants, but their efficacy was not automatic. For Huldrych Zwingli, the sacraments represented a symbolic remembrance or memorial of the continuous involvement of God's *grace in the lives of Christians. All of the aforementioned Protestants believed that faith is the condition for receiving divine enablement for one's spiritual growth and for the efficacy of the sacraments. Some Protestants do not practice sacraments per se, having a spiritualized view of grace as always available to believers. As such, Christians ought not to focus on any particular rites or rituals in aiding their spiritual growth or salvation, but rather on faith and spiritual disciplines. Examples of a spiritualized view of the sacraments include Caspar Schwenkfeld (Schwenkfelder Church), George Fox (Society of Friends), and William Booth (Salvation Army).

sacred. Anyone or anything thought to be holy, of God, or dedicated to God, and thus deserving of veneration. In the OT, *covenants, oaths, donations, vessels, and places are declared sacred. In the NT, it is noteworthy that "writings" are declared sacred: "sacred writings that are able to instruct you for salvation through faith in Christ Jesus" (2 Timothy 3:15). Sometimes the word sacred is used in contrast to objects considered secular or profane. But sacred objects are considered beneficial for people's *spiritual formation, including covenants, ceremonies, places, and especially sacred writings—*Scripture.

Sacred Heart. A religious term used especially by Catholics to symbolize the *love and *compassion of *Jesus Christ, depicted by his heart, and shown visually on his bosom in pictures and statuary. Dedication to Jesus' Sacred Heart is an important devotional practice for Catholics.

sacrifice (or self-sacrifice). The value of abstinence or self-denial of basic human needs for the sake of God. Sacrifice may serve as a spiritual discipline that enables people to focus on God and Christian *devotion. It goes far beyond practices of *frugality and *simplicity, which involve a simplified lifestyle; sacrifice involves abstention from most of life's basic human needs.

saint. One who has reached a heightened degree of spirituality. All who are saved, who have been made righteous because of *Jesus Christ's atonement, are described in *Scripture as saints (e.g., 1 Corinthians 1:2). They have been set apart for God as the church, and they are to live godly lives. In church history, Christians thought to have reached an exceptional degree of spirituality, perhaps through *martyrdom or other miraculous activities, are singled out for honor. Catholic, Orthodox, and some Protestant churches have formally canonized saints and honor them on *feast days. Whether canonized or not, historic saints have served as role models as well as inspirations for Christians today in living holy, Christlike lives.

saint, patron. A *saint believed by Catholic and Orthodox Christians who serves as a spiritual benefactor and guide for individuals, churches, regions, and even nations. Patrick went as a missionary to Ireland in the fifth century and later became Ireland's patron saint. Since saints who have died are thought

to have ascended to a heavenly existence among a *communion of saints, they continue to intercede on behalf of those
who live on earth. As saints, their prayers to God on behalf
of those for whom they are patrons are considered especially
effective *intercessions.

saints, communion of. *See* communion of saints.

salvation. The *redemption of people from *sin and death, provided by God through the atoning work of *Jesus Christ's life,
death, and resurrection. Through Jesus, people may be forgiven of their sins, become reconciled with God, and receive
*eternal life. People are believed to be saved by divine *grace
through *faith; it is a gift from God, and not a matter of human
work or merit (Ephesians 2:8-9). Scripture variously describes
how people experience salvation, involving *repentance and
faith (Mark 1:15), *baptism and receiving the gift of the Holy
*Spirit (Acts 2:38). Salvation involves more than receiving eter-
nal life; it involves a life of faithful commitment, *obedience,
and growth in relationship with God and others, based especially on God's *teachings found in *Scripture. As such, salvation is as much for this life as it is for eternal life. Christians
are encouraged by God to grow in their faith, *hope, and *love
(*see* virtues, theological), to grow in their intimacy of relationship with God, and to grow in their expressions of love to God
and to their neighbors, loving others as they love themselves.
Thus salvation marks the beginning point of renewed relationship with God, ourselves, and others, but not the ending point.
God's Spirit works continuously in helping people to *experience the fullness of divine *blessings—spiritual, physical, and
social—in store for those who are saved.

salvation, order of (Lat., *ordo salutis*). A description of the order
ordinarily thought to occur when people experience *salvation.
After the Reformation, when many Christian theological traditions emerged, Protestants talked about varying interpretations
of the order of divine *calling, *faith, *repentance, *regeneration, *justification, *assurance, *sanctification, and so on. With
regard to *spiritual formation, different views arose about the
way God works in people's lives subsequent to *conversion.
Catholics had implied an order of salvation with their emphasis

on the *sacraments as God's gracious means for spiritual formation, for example, through *baptism, *confirmation, Eucharist, reconciliation, and anointing of the sick (*see* oil, anointing with). In contrast, Protestants placed more emphasis on individual faith (and faith development) as God's gracious means for spiritual formation, especially for their sanctification.

sanctification. The biblical term used to describe God's spiritual work in the lives of believers subsequent to *conversion, restoring them to the *image of God, in which they were created. As such, sanctification has to do with the spiritual growth and service of Christians. In the OT, sanctification had to do with the setting apart of people (and objects) for the sake of making them holy. God is holy and commands that God's people be holy (e.g., Leviticus 19:2). In the NT, sanctification has to do with bringing converts into conformity with the holy righteousness of God, which was imputed to them by *grace through *justification. First Peter 1:15-16 says that Christians are to grow in *holiness and *godliness: "As he who called you is holy, be holy yourselves in all your conduct; for it is written, 'You shall be holy, for I am holy.'" Although some Christians have viewed justification and sanctification as concurrent, most consider sanctification descriptive of the ongoing work of the Holy *Spirit in the lives of believers subsequent to conversion. In this latter regard, sanctification has been thought to be a slow process of growth, depending on the transformative work of God's grace in their lives, while others believe that the Holy Spirit provides various means of grace (*see* grace, means of) for enhancing growth in righteousness, *love, and relationship with God. The latter view places greater emphasis on the synergistic partnership God intends for the process of sanctification. Although God brings about growth in holiness, God intends that people be responsible to follow biblical (and other) means of grace— sacramental and nonsacramental—that aid them in the growth process. Such voluntary aids include prayer and other *spiritual exercises, *spiritual disciplines, *gifts, and so on. Scripture mentions many of these means of grace, though others have been devised throughout church history, and have contributed to Christians' spiritual formation and maturation.

sanctification, entire. A description of the complete consecration of oneself to God, which ordinarily occurs subsequent to *conversion and results in *grace that enables one to love God with one's whole heart, *soul, mind, and strength, and one's neighbor as oneself. When the apostle Paul said: "May the God of peace himself sanctify you entirely" (1 Thessalonians 5:23), he emphasized the hope Christians have in becoming more holy, loving, Christlike. Although Christians will not experience absolute perfection in this life, John Wesley believed that they may attain a Christian *perfection (or entire sanctification) characterized by purity of intention in loving God and one's neighbor as oneself.

sanctification, initial. A reference to the sanctifying work in the lives of new converts who have been regenerated as well as justified. If justification has to do with imputed righteousness in Christians, then regeneration has to do with imparting righteousness in Christians by the presence and power of the Holy *Spirit. *Regeneration is sometimes referred to as initial sanctification.

Satan (or devil). The being in *Scripture thought to be a heavenly creature who is the archenemy of God and of the spiritual well-being of people. Satan (Heb., "the adversary," also known as the devil) appears throughout Scripture, quarreling with, accusing, and tempting people, including *Jesus Christ. In fact, Jesus carried on *spiritual warfare with Satan and *demons while on earth. Jesus warned against the "evil one," who causes *evil (Matthew 5:37), and prayed for his *disciples' protection "from the evil one" (John 17:15). Although Satan and demons continue to exist and oppress people, Christians may resist the kind of demonic possession that occurred in the NT. Spiritual warfare is variously understood by Christians. Some think that heavenly conflict occurs continuously between Satan, demons, and *angels, and that our lives are directly affected by the outcome; others think that the power of Satan and demons has more to do with influencing, tempting, and persuading people to act sinfully, contrary to God. Throughout church history, Christians have believed that resistance to Satan and demons is critical for their spiritual and, indeed, their holistic well-being.

Thus the evil influence of Satan and demons ought not to be ignored or underestimated when pursuing *spiritual formation and Christian living.

Scripture (or Scriptures). Known as the "writing, or writings," and also known as the Bible, or the "book," the Scriptures are sacred writings considered to be divinely revealed by God. Second Timothy 3:16 describes all Scripture as inspired by God, literally "God breathed," and "useful for teaching, for reproof, for correction, and for training in righteousness." Second Peter 1:20-21 says that all Scriptures are inspired by the Holy *Spirit. Christianity divides its Scriptures into two parts, or testaments: Old Testament (Hebrew Scriptures) and New Testament (Christian Scriptures). These testaments represent another way to contrast the two covenants talked about by *Jesus and his followers (e.g., Hebrews 8:8; 9:15). Both the OT and NT are valued for how they aid people in their *spiritual formation as well as for their knowledge of God and for their *salvation.

Scripture, meditation on. *See* lectio divina.

Scripture, rereading. Rereading *Scripture from a particular perspective, for example, spiritual formation, advocacy for the poor, or concern for justice. Sometimes reading Scripture anew, looking for insights from Scripture previously overlooked, can bring profound learning and growth. Rereading Scripture for the sake of *spiritual formation can benefit people's self-awareness and actions in becoming more *Christlike. The rereading of Scripture often takes place in Third World countries, where Christians try to understand their beliefs and values, as well as their spiritual practices, from their own sociocultural context.

secrecy (or confidentiality). The value of discretion, maintaining public reserve, and confidentiality, which may have to do with sensitive information about oneself or others. Secrecy may serve as a *spiritual discipline that enables people to focus on God and Christian *devotion, and not to divulge information about oneself or others that is best kept private.

See You at the Pole. Public prayer event, held near a flagpole, for example, at a school or civic event.

self-control. The ability to regulate oneself, aided by divine *grace. Self-control is especially useful for spiritual growth and is considered one manifestation of the *fruit of the Spirit. Related to self-control is the virtue of *temperance, also known as moderation.

self-examination. Critical self-analysis of oneself, especially of one's relationship with God and of one's spiritual well-being. *Scripture talks about the importance of examining oneself, which helps to lead one to God and to godly living (e.g., Lamentations 3:40; 1 Corinthians 11:27-28). The daily *examen is an example of regular, prayerful self-examination.

semi-Augustinianism. The theology affirming that God voluntarily restricts God's power over people in order that they may make free, responsible choices with regard to their *salvation and to their spiritual formation. Semi-Augustinianism arose in response to Augustinianism and characterizes most theologies in church history, including Catholic, Orthodox, Anglican, and many Protestant Christians (e.g., Arminians, Wesleyans, *Pentecostals). As such, God gives people *grace preveniently, which calls, enables, and completes their decision making. People may voluntarily resist God's grace, which is why there is sin. However, the Holy *Spirit graciously works in the lives of people in order to aid them in their salvation and godly Christian living. *See also* Augustinianism.

senses (sensate spirituality). The faculties by which people experience sight, sound, touch, taste, and smell; they are thought to be inextricably bound up with people's spiritual faculties. The senses are a part of our physical reality, which God created, and which will be a part of our *resurrected bodies. In church history, Christians have been divided with regard to the role of senses in relationship to their spirituality. On the one hand, some have considered the senses (including affections desires, passions, and appetites) to distract from spirituality, especially due to humanity's fall into *sin (e.g., Galatians 5:24). As such, *ascetic practices were encouraged historically in order to purge oneself from fleshly appetites and *temptations that pull one away from God and godly behavior. On the other hand, others have considered the senses as faculties that contribute to other human faculties, including the rational and spiritual dimensions of human existence. For example, there may be a sensate "hunger and thirst" for God's righteousness (Matthew 5:6). As such, it is good and beneficial to affirm human senses, and their contribution to *spiritual formation, sacramental *worship, and other forms of Christian service. Thus a kind of sensate spirituality not only affirms human senses but also glories in exploring them in life, in the natural world, and other expressions of this-worldly beauty, *art, and *music, which embody both natural and supernatural significance.

Serenity Prayer. A prayer attributed to the twentieth-century theologian Reinhold Niebuhr, intended to aid in one's holistic well-being. Although the prayer has appeared with various wordings, the following is a well-known version: "God, grant me the serenity to accept the things I cannot change, the courage to change the things I can, and the wisdom to know the difference." The prayer has been popular among Christians, in recovery networks such as *twelve-step programs, and also for *spiritual formation. The prayer petitions God for serenity, *courage, and *wisdom in helping people make responsible decisions for their holistic well-being. Spiritually, the prayer has aided people with regard to their spiritual formation and Christian living.

servant. A person who renders *service to another in tangible ways, and in Christianity, service to God. In the OT, the prophets spoke of the coming Messiah as a servant, and *Jesus Christ described himself as the servant of all by ministering to his *disciples, obeying God's will, and dying on the cross (e.g., Luke 22:27). Christians are to emulate Jesus, especially if they desire to become spiritually *Christlike in their service to God and to others.

service. Aid to others, usually in tangible ways through expressions of *compassion or advocacy. Service may function as a *spiritual discipline that enables people to focus on God and Christian devotion.

service (or serving), gift of. A special enabling of the Holy *Spirit that empowers believers to serve others self-sacrificially.

sex, sexuality. An act of physical intimacy or that which relates, literally or figuratively, to sex. Sexual relations have been thought to help and also hinder *spiritual formation. Within the bounds of biblical teachings, sexual relations are thought to be a good and spiritually healthy expression of *marriage between men and women, conducive to their spiritual as well as physical well-being. Sexuality also functions as an analogy for the intimacy available between people and God (e.g., Song of Songs). *Mystics throughout church history, for example, have found sexual language useful in promoting *spiritual formation. However, sexual relations have been considered detrimental when they distract or tempt people away from God, biblical morality, and spiritual priorities.

shalom. The Hebrew word for *peace, which also communicates wholeness—spiritually, physically, and socially. Shalom continues to be used by Christians in communicating the breadth and depth of peace that God intends for people to *experience. As such, it also is used to describe the holistic dimension of one's spiritual well-being, and so shalom is a goal of *spiritual formation. Consequently, shalom is increasingly used as a greeting among Christians.

Shema. The Hebrew word for "hear," which is the first word of the famous Jewish prayer: "Hear, O Israel: The LORD is our God, the LORD alone. You shall love the LORD your God with all your heart, and with all your soul, and with all your might" (Deuteronomy 6:4-5). Jesus Christ used these words as the starting point in describing the greatest commandment (Mark 12:28-31). The Shema demonstrates that *love has always been at the core of Christianity, in both the OT and NT, and thus also of Christian spirituality.

shepherding, gift of. A special enabling of the Holy *Spirit that empowers believers to nurture or pastor others.

silence. The value of quietness and calm composure, especially for the sake of people's spiritual well-being. Silence may serve as a *spiritual discipline that enables people to focus on God and Christian *devotion. Silence may often include *solitude, which is another spiritual discipline.

simplicity. The value of minimizing or making things easier, reducing complications, especially for the sake of one's spiritual well-being. Simplicity may serve as a *spiritual discipline that enables people to focus on God and Christian *devotion (e.g., 1 Peter 3:4). Simplicity may include *frugality and thriftiness.

sin. Betrayal of God, which occurs by transgression of God's laws, by faithless rejection, or passive indifference toward relationship with God. Sin is thought to be the prime spiritual predicament separating humankind from a right relationship with God (e.g., Isaiah 59:2). It has left humankind bereft of God's favor, and made them culpable of judgment and damnation, separating forever sinners from God (e.g., 2 Thessalonians 1:8-10). After the original fall of humanity into sin, people are thought to have a propensity to sin inherited from their forebears. However, because of the atonement of *Jesus Christ, people may be saved from judgment and damnation due to sin, and they may be reconciled with God forever. Because of the presence and power of the Holy *Spirit, believers may grow spiritually, overcome sin, and be increasingly restored to the image of God in which they originally were created. Of course, people are challenged in life by more than sin. As finite human beings, they also suffer from ignorance, misery of various sorts, and bondage—both spiritual and physical. For example, people struggle with ignorance of the importance of spiritual matters and the ways in which they need to grow spiritually. They may struggle with various kinds of physical, mental, emotional, and other types of misery, which influence their spiritual well-being. People may also struggle due to various forms of bondage to *Satan or demonic presences in their lives, who seek spiritually to oppress or, if possible, possess them. Other bondages exist, for example, addictive habits or obsessions that bind people and thus thwart their spiritual well-being. Finally, sin remains the prime challenge to living holy and spiritually vital lives, and yet Christians are hopeful because God's *grace enables them to overcome sin.

sing, singing. Vocalizing words and sound in melody, harmony, and other musical expressions, for the sake of spiritual acclamation. People may sing as a way to *praise and thank God, or to make other expressions that function as public, worshipful, and celebrative prayers. In addition to singing prayers, people may also sing *Scripture, *liturgy, or other devotional aids. Like *prayer, singing may be individual or corporate, silent or vocal, liturgical or extemporaneous. Singing is thought especially expressive of spiritual joy and *celebration. *See also* music; song, spiritual.

sins, seven deadly. Seven sins deemed by medieval Christians to be especially damaging to one's spiritual life. They include lust, gluttony, greed, sloth, wrath, envy, and pride. The seven deadly sins contrast with seven *virtues, which include chastity, *temperance, charity (*see* love), diligence, *patience, kindness, and *humility. For *spiritual formation and flourishing Christian living, it is as important to resist the seven deadly sins as it is to pursue the seven virtues.

solitude. The value of being alone or separating oneself from the clamor of life, especially for the sake of one's spiritual well-being. Solitude may serve as a *spiritual discipline that enables people to focus on God and Christian *devotion. Solitude may include *silence, which is another one of the spiritual disciplines.

song, spiritual. Any song conveying spiritual meaning about God and matters related to God. *Scripture talks about singing "psalms and hymns and spiritual songs" (Ephesians 5:19). Spiritual songs include *hymns, choruses, poems, or anything else sung to the glory and praise of God. The *singing of songs can be very helpful to one's spiritual flourishing alone or with others, as well as to one's honoring God.

soul. The essence of oneself, which has been variously understood by both Christians and non-Christians, and is inextricably related to one's spiritual well-being. *Scripture sometimes talks about people as having a body and soul (e.g., Matthew 10:28), in which the soul pertains to their spirituality; other times Scripture talks about people as having a body, soul, and spirit (e.g., 1 Thessalonians 5:23), in which the soul pertains to the capacity for perception, feeling, and volition. As such, spirit is sometime identified with the soul (e.g., Luke 1:46-47), and at other times they are contrasted (e.g., Hebrews 4:12). So, in some sense, use of the word *soul* may have more to do with a unified—albeit complex—understanding of the self. From this perspective, it would be more appropriate to call a person a soul, than to say that a person has a soul. In ancient Greece, the soul was thought to be incorporeal and immortal, enlivening one's physical body. Some Christians continued this understanding of the soul, claiming it to be immortal; other Christians did not consider the soul to be innately immortal but needing *resurrection (along with the physical body) for *eternal life. A contemporary view of the soul argues for nonreductive physicalism, which conceives of people physically but with their totality transcending mere physicality. Regardless of one's view of the soul, Christians continue to affirm the reality and importance of the spiritual dimension of people's lives and how it ought to be cared for both through *salvation and subsequent *spiritual formation.

Soul of Christ (Lat., *Anima Christi*). A medieval, Christ-centered prayer that has been used by the Catholic Church to begin *Mass. *Anima Christi* is a *petitionary prayer for spiritual transformation by and relationship with *Jesus Christ, and occurs at the beginning of *Ignatian spiritual exercises.

space, sacred. Any space thought to be beneficial for one's relationship with God, for worshiping God, and for growing spiritually. For individuals, sacred space may be a place where they can go to pray, read *Scripture, or participate in other *spiritual disciplines. Sacred space may also be in public places such as church or a place of beauty that inspires them spiritually. For collective groups of Christians, church structures have been a common sacred space—a place built and prepared, sometimes elaborately—for *worship, *teaching, and ministry to others. Other public spaces that are sacred may include cities to which pilgrimages are made, thought to be conducive to inspiring people spiritually. *See also* time, sacred.

spirit. That which is immaterial, spiritual, or divine; both *God and people are described as spirit. God is said to be spirit, and true *worship of God occurs in spirit and truth (John 4:24). Throughout the OT, God's Spirit abides in people, rests on them, is put in them, and is poured out on them. In the NT, the Holy *Spirit represents God's primary presence and involvement in the lives of people. In some instances, people are described as a dichotomy: body and spirit (e.g., Matthew 10:28), whereas at other times they are described as a trichotomy: body, soul, and spirit (e.g., 1 Thessalonians 5:23). Spirit is sometime identified with the *soul (e.g., Luke 1:46-47), while at other times they are contrasted (e.g., Hebrews 4:12). Spirit is often thought to be a part of what it means to be created in the *image of God. Care for the human spirit is thought to be essential to Christian spirituality. Sometimes reference to people's spirit has to do with the quality of their character or spirituality. A broken or contrite spirit is commended, while a haughty spirit is chastised. Jesus said that the *kingdom of God belongs to those who are poor in spirit (Matthew 5:3). God promised to put a new spirit within people, and they should seek to be filled with God's Spirit (Ephesians 5:18). Not every spirit is to be believed (1 John 4:1). Indeed there are worldly beliefs and values to which people become enslaved, as well as unclean and demonic spirits in the world.

Spirit, filled with the (or Spirit-filled). A biblical reference to those especially empowered and controlled by the Holy *Spirit for Christian living. Such in-filling is thought to aid people in their *spiritual formation, *obedience to God, and witness to others. Christians are exhorted to be "filled with the Spirit" (Ephesians 5:18).

Spirit, full of the. A biblical reference to the ongoing character of being filled with the *Spirit. Some Christians are described as being mature and "full of the Spirit" as well as having other spiritual *virtues (e.g., Acts 6:3-5).

Spirit, Holy. God's Spirit, revealed in *Scripture as the third personal manifestation of the one *God, and who is divine, holy, and individual, in relation to God the Father and God the Son, Jesus Christ (*see* Trinity). The Holy Spirit was sent to work among people the world over, after Jesus' ascension, at the time of Pentecost. Now the Holy Spirit acts as God's primary presence in the world, working in and through the lives of people, especially Christians. With regard to spirituality, the Holy Spirit works to call people to *salvation, to aid them graciously for their salvation, and then to empower them for growth in spirituality, *Christlikeness, *holiness, *love, and *service to others. The Holy Spirit gives people the *fruit of the

Spirit (e.g., Galatians 5:22-23), *gifts (e.g., 1 Corinthians 12:7-11), and other empowerment for Christian living. It is not enough for people to be *justified; the Holy Spirit works to *sanctify people entirely (e.g., 1 Thessalonians 5:23). Other ways that the Holy Spirit aids people in their spiritual lives is to assure them of salvation, intercede on their behalf, and spiritually in-fill them so that they become "full of the Holy Spirit" (Acts 11:24; cf. Luke 4:1).

Spirit, in the. *Scripture talks about living "in the Spirit," sometimes contrasted with living life under the control of the flesh—of nonspiritual, ungodly influences (e.g., Romans 8:9). Similarly, Christians talk about walking in the Spirit, emphasizing the need to submit to God's Spirit and be open to God's working in and through individuals and groups (e.g., Galatians 5:16). Those who live or walk in the Spirit are thought to have achieved a heightened state of spirituality, being attentive to God and avoiding *sin.

spiritual. That which is of an immaterial, spirit-oriented, or divine nature. From a Christian perspective, things of a spiritual nature have to do with people's relationship with God, or more specifically, the Holy Spirit of God. As such, being spiritual has to do with loving God with all of one's heart, *soul, mind, and strength, and also loving one's neighbor as oneself. Other ways of describing people's spiritual lives has to do with life in the Spirit (e.g., Romans 8:9), God dwelling in humans (e.g., 1 Corinthians 3:16), and walking in the Spirit (e.g., Galatians. 5:16). *Scripture describes many things as being spiritual, such as the *law, *gifts, *blessings, *wisdom, and more.

spiritual direction. Guidance for the sake of spiritual growth. It occurs generally through the direction of churches or church leadership, but it may also occur individually through a *mentor or *spiritual director. Indeed, there is no end to the ways in which one may receive spiritual direction. But those interested in receiving spiritual direction consider the experience and *maturity of individuals specifically dedicated to serving as a mentor or spiritual director to be the most effective in aiding them.

spiritual director. One who guides and mentors others spiritually, one on one or in small groups. In *Scripture, individuals mentor others individually (e.g., Elijah and Elisha) and collectively (e.g., *Jesus and the *disciples). Over time, spiritual directors functioned through clergy and lay leaders, who considered it their *vocation. Today Christians may serve formally as spiritual directors after receiving training and certification for giving spiritual guidance to others.

spiritual disciplines. Practices, exercises, or *habits people perform to facilitate spiritual development, enabled by God's grace. *Scripture mentions a variety of things that people may do which beneficially prepare them for God's gracious work in their lives. Spiritual disciplines are not ways by which people initiate spiritual growth, but they are ways God has provided for people to respond to or cooperate with divine *grace for transformation into *Christlikeness. *Asceticism has sometimes been associated with spiritual disciplines, but the former is considered more intense and usually requires self-denial, including separation of some sort from others and society for the sake of purgation (*see* purification). Spiritual disciplines are thought to be accessible to people at all times and places. Historically, Christians have categorized spiritual disciplines in various ways. For example, Richard Foster distinguishes between inward disciplines (*prayer, *study, *fasting, *meditation), outward disciplines (*solitude, *simplicity, submission, *service), and corporate disciplines (*worship, *celebration, guidance, *confession). Dallas Willard distinguishes between disciplines of engagement (prayer, study, worship, celebration, submission, confession, service, *fellowship) and disciplines of abstinence (solitude, *silence, fasting, *frugality, chastity, *secrecy, *sacrifice). Other spiritual disciplines practiced by Christians include *sacraments, *self-examination, *spiritual direction, holy friendships, covenant groups, *hospitality, *relaxation exercises, *rule of life, prayer of *examen, *journaling, and so on. Practically speaking, many aids, practices, or exercises may be useful means of grace (*see* grace, means of) by which God transforms people into Christlikeness, and Christians have felt free to experiment in developing disciplines conducive to *spiritual formation.

spiritual exercises. A general reference to practiced trainings for the sake of growth in relationship with God, in spirituality, or in Christian living. Most often spiritual exercises are identified with *spiritual disciplines, all of which are enabled by divine *grace. Spiritual exercises are often associated with a multi-week program of prayer developed by *Ignatius of Loyola.

spiritual exercises of Ignatius. A multiweek program of *prayer, *fasting, and activities with a *spiritual director. The program consists of spiritual exercises *Ignatius of Loyola developed in the sixteenth century order to help Christians experience spiritual *freedom and deepen their commitment to God. Ignatius separated the exercises into four "weeks" (which may be literal weeks or phases) that meditate on *Jesus Christ's life and call for Christians to become *disciples. In practicing the spiritual exercises, Ignatius emphasized two forms of prayer: *meditation and *contemplation. The daily *examen served as an important spiritual exercise designed for conquering and regulating one's life in order to contemplate God. Another prayer used in Ignatius's spiritual exercises begins with the words "Take, Lord, and receive," known by the Latin word *suscipe* (Lat., "receive"), in consecrating oneself to God.

spiritual formation. The spiritual nurture of believers by God's grace through their *faith, *hope, *love, and other spiritual *virtues. Formation (Lat., *formatio*) has been a long-standing emphasis among Christians, believing that *Scripture commands and encourages the discipling of others for the sake of their spiritual well-being, facilitated by divine grace through faithful obedience. Faithful participation includes *prayer and other spiritual practices (exercises, disciplines) described in Scripture and developed throughout church history.

spiritual warfare. Christian spirituality represents a conflict or struggle between spiritual beings, including both human and celestial beings, such as *angels and *demons. *Jesus actively confronted *Satan and demonic beings (Matthew 4:10; Luke 11:14-23). Angelic beings aided people, directly and indirectly (Matthew 4:11; John 1:51). In *Scripture, sometimes spiritual warfare occurs between angelic and demonic beings, and sometimes spiritual warfare occurs between demonic beings and people. Regardless, people are believed to be affected by the outcome of the warfare. Although demons may possess

people, as they do in Scripture, it is thought that the most demons can do against Christians is to oppress them. But such
demonic influence ought not to be minimized in its effects on
the spiritual well-being of Christians. Thus *spiritual formation requires attentiveness to and *prayer in support of spiritual warfare against all forces of *evil, celestial or terrestrial
(Ephesians 6:12).

spiritualism. A belief that advocates contact with those who
have died, either individually or by means of trained special-
ists or mediums. Saul asked a medium to bring the spirit of
Samuel back to life—a deed for which Saul was condemned
(1 Chronicles 10:13-14). *Scripture denounces mediums as well
(Leviticus 20:27).

spirituality. That which has to do with spirit or spiritual matters, especially with people's relationship with God. As such,
spirituality has to do with the quality of our relationship with
God, especially *love for God, and intimacy of *union and communing with God. In the English language, the word *spirituality* is a relatively new word, first appearing in print in the early
twentieth century. But the word is thought to communicate a
long-standing emphasis on a right and loving relationship with
God, as found in *Scripture. However, in Scripture, matters of
spirituality are usually described as spirit, having a spirit, life
in the spirit, fallen spirit, renewed spirit, and spirit beyond
death. Spirituality also pertains to all so-called supernatural
dimensions of life and nature, or with spiritual beings, and
people's relationship to them. There are different types of spirituality, which can be studied historically and scientifically:
Christian and non-Christian, religious and secular, individual
and corporate, relational and philosophical, and so on.

stations of the cross (or way of the cross). Images that depict
circumstances related to the crucifixion of Jesus Christ, and
the prayerful reflections that Christians have in *meditation
on each event depicted. Usually fourteen images, made up of
paintings, reliefs, sculptures, or *crosses, are placed in churches or pathways. Individuals or groups of individuals may walk
from image to image in honor of the *passion of Jesus' sacrifice for them and for how they may emulate his exemplary life.

Most often Christians observe the stations of the cross during *Lent and Good Friday. The events of Jesus' crucifixion originally occurred in Jerusalem on what is known as the *Via Dolorosa* (Lat., "way of grief" or "way of sorrows").

story. An account or narrative, especially told for the purpose of enabling those who hear it to envision spiritual meaning and practical implications for those who hear the story. Stories may be historical or allegorical (symbolic), such as a fable or parable. They appear throughout *Scripture and among Christians' spiritual pursuits in church history. The use of stories has become more prominent nowadays due to the growing emphasis on a postmodern worldview, in which people utilize a narrative approach to understanding truth, including spiritual truth.

studious spirituality. A type of spirituality that emphasizes study, especially the study of *Scripture, but also of other Christian literature, especially spiritual literature. Participation in Bible study and other Christian studies is considered a heightened expression of Christian spirituality. Examples of studious spirituality include the apologetics of Irenaeus of Lyons and Clement of Alexandria, the trinitarian scholarship of the Cappadocian fathers, and the scholastic theology of Anselm of Canterbury and Thomas Aquinas. Historically, study has been considered a *spiritual discipline, especially the study of Scripture by Christians from all church traditions.

study. Learning and thinking, especially done for the purpose of understanding Christian spirituality and its development. Study is indispensable to Christianity, for example, when *Jesus Christ said that believers are to love God with their minds as well as their heart, *soul, and strength (Mark 12:29-30). Study of God's *law is important (Ezra 7:10), and people in Berea are commended for examining the *Scriptures every day in order to assess the truthfulness of claims made by the apostle Paul (Acts 17:10-11). Study includes the investigation and defense (apologetics) of Scripture, but it includes interdisciplinary study as well, especially those studies conducive to *spiritual formation.

suffering. Physical pain and spiritual anguish; the word is used by Christians to describe the pain and anguish *Jesus Christ suffered during his humiliation and crucifixion on the *cross. In Latin, "suffering" is known as *passio*, and thus Christians refer to the "*passion" of Christ and to the celebration of Holy Week before *Easter as Passion Week. Some Christians in church history have employed suffering as an *ascetic practice in the aid of *obedience to God and of *spiritual formation, including extreme practices (e.g., *flagellation).

suffering, prayer in. Prayer that occurs in the midst of *suffering, or suffering that serves as prayer. It may occur as a *lament of pain and grief or a *petition, requesting compassionate aid or advocacy on behalf of one's suffering.

Sunday. The first day of the week, on which early Christians gathered for worship (e.g., Acts 20:7-8). Public worship on Sundays distinguished Christians from Jewish worship. The former honored the resurrection of Jesus Christ on Sunday, rather than observing the traditional Sabbath, which extended from sundown on Friday through sundown on Saturday. *Scripture exhorts Christians to develop the *habit of regularly gathering together, for example, for worship services (e.g., Hebrews 10:24-25). Historically, Sunday worship services have been invaluable for the spiritual nurture of Christians.

supplication. Fervent petition, particularly *petitionary prayer. Supplication has to do with the supplicant asking or begging God in prayer a question or request, or about a particular concern.

symbols. Signs or images useful for spiritual reflection and growth. Symbols are used by Christians to focus on God or spiritual matters. For example, some find it spiritually beneficial to reflect or meditate on religious symbols, such as the *cross; sacramental elements of *water, *bread, and *wine; *icons; and so on. Religious *art and statuary are also considered beneficial for *spiritual formation.

T

Taizé. An international and ecumenical Christian community that organized monastically in Taizé, France. Composed of Catholics and Protestants, the community appeals especially to young people who are committed to *prayer, *teaching, Bible study, and ministry to the poor. Spiritually, they emphasize lives of *simplicity, *celibacy, and *reconciliation.

teaching. The act of instruction for the spiritual development of Christians. Instruction is essential for *spiritual formation; *Jesus Christ taught his *disciples, and exhorted them to teach all nations "to obey everything that I have commanded you" (Matthew 28:20). The Holy *Spirit reminds people of Jesus' teachings and leads them into new insight. Paul told Christians to teach and admonish one another. *Scripture refers to teaching, or being a teacher, as one of the *gifts of the Holy Spirit.

temperance. The self-control of thoughts, words, and actions that aids one's spiritual well-being. Historically, temperance is considered one of the cardinal virtues (*see* virtues, cardinal). As such, it represents the cultivation of knowing how far to go without going too far, also known as moderation. Temperance aids spirituality inasmuch as people need to be sensible and moderate in how they understand and go about *spiritual formation. The temperance movement advocated abstinence from alcoholic beverages because of the addictive nature of alcoholism.

temptation. Enticement to do that which is against the will or laws of God. Those who *sin by succumbing to temptation need to *repent; those who withstand the test of temptation receive God's *blessings (James 1:12). According to James, God does not tempt people (James 1:13-15); instead, they are tempted by their own desires. Christians believe that God graciously aids them in overcoming temptation through *prayer and other means of grace (*see* grace, means of).

testimony. The sharing of one's *story, often of what God has done in one's *salvation and spiritual well-being. Testimonies, or testimonials, may serve as effective ways to verbalize the *blessings of God, and they may serve as inspiration to others. Often included in testimonies are the challenges in a person's life and the request for *prayer. Testimony services allow groups of people to tell about their spiritual journeys, edifying one another. Testimonies may also serve as ways to proclaim the *gospel message of Jesus Christ.

thanksgiving. The giving of gratitude and due recognition to God in both word and deed. Thanksgiving represents an important expression of Christian *prayer. Believers are admonished to give thanks to God, and they are to give offerings of thanksgiving to God. God is to be thanked for all that has been given, and *petitions to God are to be made with thanksgiving.

thanksgiving prayer. Prayer focused on giving thanks. Thanksgiving prayers are especially directed toward God, for God's blessings in general, or for specific blessings of a spiritual, physical, or social nature.

theosis. The aim of Christian *maturity, of *godliness, by which believers become like God by sharing in the divine nature (e.g., 2 Peter 1:4). Orthodox churches use the Greek word *theōsis* (deification, divinization) in order to emphasize their confidence in the *grace of God to transform people, especially by their participation in *spiritual disciplines. They do not mean that believers can become divine but that divine grace may transform people into greater *Christlikeness, *holiness, and *perfection. In Orthodox traditions, theosis is believed to be attainable by all Christians, whereas Catholics believe that such holiness is limited to those who follow counsels of perfection (*see* perfection, counsels of).

time, sacred. A time (or regular time occurrences) thought to be especially favorable for spiritual and religious matters. Sacred time may occur anytime persons sense that God is present, working in and through their lives; sacred time may also include regularly scheduled activities that promote *spiritual formation. For example, times of the day are set aside for *prayer or meditative study (e.g., *Hours); times of the week are set aside for public *worship or for *service; times of the month are set aside for sacramental observances or ministerial outreach; and times of the year are set aside for celebrative *holy days, *feast days, or for other religious commemorations. In seeking conditions favorable for spiritual healing and growth, people establish a rhythm or cycle of times that are especially favorable for them in prayer and other *spiritual disciplines. *See also* space, sacred.

tongues, gift of. A special enabling of the Holy *Spirit that empowers believers to speak in a language unknown to the speaker. Tongues speaking may occur either as heavenly tongues (a personal language given to believers by which they can communicate directly with God) or earthly tongues previously unknown to the believer. As with other *gifts of the Spirit, the gift can be temporary, given for a specific reason on a specific occasion, or it can be a gift readily available to the believer at any time. *Pentecostals believe that earthly tongues are given for occasional use, while heavenly tongues are given for continual use. The gift of tongues is controversial among *cessationists, who believe that gifts such as tongues ceased after the apostolic age, and that current manifestations of tongues are either psychological or demonic manifestations. *Continuationists believe that all gifts of the Spirit, including tongues speaking, continue to be used by God to build up the *church and to minister to those outside churches.

tongues, interpretation of. The translation or explanation of speaking in tongues. The interpretation of tongues is described as a *gift of the Holy *Spirit (1 Corinthians 12:10, 30), just as is speaking in tongues. The interpretation of tongues may involve discernment, which is also described as a gift of the Holy Spirit (1 Corinthians 12:10). Some *Pentecostals think that tongues speaking ought not to occur publicly unless there is someone to interpret, whereas others encourage speaking in tongues, regardless of whether there is someone to interpret. Someone other than those speaking in tongues may interpret, or those speaking in tongues may interpret the words or meaning themselves.

tongues, interpretation of, gift of. A special enabling of the Holy *Spirit that empowers believers to interpret tongues speaking.

tongues, speaking in (or tongues speaking). Speech or prayer by Christians in an unknown language. Tongues speaking is described in *Scripture as *glōssolalia* (Gk., *glōssa*, "tongue, language" + *laleo*, "speak, talk, make a sound"). It is described as one of the spiritual *gifts. Speaking in tongues occurred at *Pentecost, when the Holy *Spirit gave followers of *Jesus the ability to speak in other languages (Acts 2:4). Tongues speaking was considered a fulfillment of Joel 2:28-32, which prophesied that God's Spirit would be poured out on all people. The event of Pentecost has been interpreted differently by Christians; for example, some consider the speaking in tongues to be known languages, while others consider them unknown or angelic languages (1 Corinthians 13:1). Still others consider tongues speaking to be a psychological or, perhaps, demonic phenomenon. Tongues speaking is thought by many Pentecostals to be the visible or physical evidence of *baptism with (or in) the Holy Spirit (e.g., Acts 1:5; 2:4; 11:16). Pentecostal (and also *charismatic) Christians consider Pentecost a paradigmatic event for all believers, who also have the privilege of experiencing Holy Spirit baptism subsequent to conversion. Pentecostals do not always agree whether tongues speaking represents prayer to God, or whether it also includes communication from God to believers. Others consider speaking in tongues more of a private *prayer language for the spiritual edification of the individual (1 Corinthians 14:4). Regardless, tongues speaking is thought to represent a heightened state of Christian spirituality, the means by which to grow closer to God and be empowered for Christian prayer, living, and ministry.

tradition, traditions. A reference to the beliefs, values, and practices passed on from forebears, especially those of spiritual import. In *Scripture, a distinction is made between the tradition (or traditions) of people and the tradition passed on by God or by God's authoritative representatives, such as the *disciples and the writers of *Scripture. In church history, a single tradition (or Tradition) of Christianity has been uplifted to describe the authoritative view of Christianity (e.g., Catholic and Orthodox churches). Protestants disagreed, instead arguing that there existed multiple valid traditions. Spiritually, people have benefited from the variety of traditions of *spiritual formation, though those traditions thought to trace back to Scripture have generally been considered superior to those that arose in church history.

transfiguration. A reference to the transfiguration of *Jesus Christ in the NT, in which he went up a mountain with several *disciples and began to shine with light while meeting Moses and Elijah (e.g., Matthew 17:1-9). The transfiguration has multiple levels of meaning, emphasizing the affirmation of Jesus by God, of Jesus' superior authority to speak for God, and of the certainty of *resurrection. Spiritually, the images of light and transfiguration have been used to talk about the light of *grace in guiding people's lives, and of transfiguring (or transforming) them into greater *Christlikeness.

trial. That which tests a person's character and quality of spirituality. In *Scripture, people may be tested by *Satan (and *demons), who *tempts them to sin. Generally, Christians contrast trials and temptations, since God may test people in order to strengthen their *faith, *hope, and *love (e.g., Hebrews 12:7; James 1:2-4).

trinitarian formula. Any reference to the Father, Son, and Holy Spirit, which alludes to the biblical doctrine of the *Trinity, used for theological and spiritual reasons. The wording comes, for example, from baptismal phraseology in Matthew 28:19: "in the name of the Father and of the Son and of the Holy Spirit." Any reference to Father, Son, and Holy Spirit, including inclusive-language variations, is considered a trinitarian formula.

Trinity. The belief or doctrine that there is one God who exists mysteriously as three persons. The Trinity is not so much an explanation of God as it is a statement about the limits of our knowledge of God as revealed in *Scripture. Scripture reveals God as one, yet it also refers to God the Father, God the Son, and God the Holy *Spirit as separate and equally divine persons. Spiritually, the Trinity has been important for Christians and churches throughout church history. Christian *rites and *rituals have been deeply influenced by the Trinity, representing the holistic ways in which God continues to work in our lives. Sacramentally, the *trinitarian formula of Father, Son, and Holy Spirit (Matthew 28:19) is considered essential for *baptism as well as for other church rites and *liturgy. Such biblical wording is so important that many churches insist on using this trinitarian formula, despite growing inclusive references to the Trinity, such as Creator, Redeemer, and Sanctifier. Relationally, the Trinity demonstrates the eternal *love between Father, Son, and Holy Spirit, and the centrality of love to God's nature. Love represents the essence of spiritual well-being, particularly in people's love for God and for their neighbors as themselves.

twelve-step spirituality. The step-by-step guidelines used for helping people recover from various addictions, which some consider spiritual guidelines that depend on a "higher power" or "loving God." Originating in the 1939 book *Alcoholics Anonymous*, the twelve steps help individuals overcome alcoholism (and other addictions) through a program of recovery that includes group accountability. People have also used the twelve-step program as foundational for their spiritual self-understanding and for growth.

U

union with Christ. The spiritual bond or communion that people experience in relationship with *Jesus Christ. The apostle Paul speaks of communion with all three persons of the Trinity in 2 Corinthians 13:13: "The grace of the Lord Jesus Christ, the love of God, and the communion of the Holy Spirit be with all of you." Some Christians consider union with Christ to be generally descriptive of *salvation and the *reconciliation between people and God (e.g., Romans 8:1; Galatians 3:26-28). However, other Christians consider union (or communion) with Christ to be the most personal and spiritually intimate experience that people may have with God. Christian *mystics describe union with God as the highest experience of intimacy with God, which may include *ecstatic or trancelike experiences.

unitive way. A mystical approach to Christian spirituality that promotes *union (or communion) with God. In *mysticism, union with God represented the culmination of three stages of spiritual enlightenment: *purification (purgative way), *meditation (illuminative way), and union with God (unitive way).

V

Vespers. The evening office, or service of prayer, conducted after the evening meal and before bedtime in many liturgical churches, including Catholic, Orthodox, Anglican, and Lutheran churches. As a sung service in the Anglican tradition, it is called Evensong.

via media **(Lat., "middle way").** A phrase used by Anglicans to describe their intent to be a middle way between the Roman Catholic Church and the Protestant churches in continental Europe. Not only theologically and ecclesiastically but also spiritually, Anglican churches wanted to create a middle way between the two church *traditions, preserving the best of both.

Virgin Mary. One of the titles of Mary the mother of Jesus, often used liturgically for spiritual inspiration in Catholic and Orthodox churches. The Orthodox also use the term Ever-Virgin in affirming her perpetual virginity.

virtue. Behavior demonstrating excellence in character, including spiritual excellence. Virtue derives from the Greek word *aretē*, which means an "excellence" of any kind. Christians thought of *faith, *hope, and *love as theological virtues (*see* virtues, theological; 1 Corinthians 13:13). Medieval Christians adopted Greek virtues as cardinal virtues (*see* virtues, cardinal), which included prudence (*see* wisdom), *temperance, *justice, and *courage. They complemented the theological virtues for the sake of flourishing spiritually. Over time, other excellences have been emphasized, such as intellectual virtues. Indeed, long lists of virtues have been created in talking about the many excellences in life. For Christians, the development of virtue has been considered a beneficial understanding of *spiritual formation, vital to flourishing in Christian living.

virtues, cardinal. The medieval affirmation of four Greek *virtues: prudence (*wisdom), *temperance (moderation), *justice, and *courage. The cardinal virtues are thought to be complementary both to biblical teachings and particularly to the theological virtues of *faith, *hope, and *love (*see* virtues, theological). Virtues exist both as gifts of divine *grace and as qualities of excellence that need to be developed.

virtues, seven (seven heavenly virtues). Seven excellences in character, identified by medieval Christians as important for flourishing in biblical, Christlike living. The seven virtues include chastity, *temperance, charity, diligence, *patience, kindness, and *humility. They contrast with the seven deadly sins of lust, gluttony, greed, sloth, wrath, envy, and pride. These lists of virtues and vices aid Christians in focusing on growing into *Christlikeness.

virtues, theological. The biblical excellences of *faith, *hope, and *love mentioned by Paul in 1 Corinthians 13:13. Christians in the early church talked about faith, hope, and love as virtues. Virtues in general, and the theological virtues in particular, exist both as gifts of divine *grace and as qualities of excellence that need to be developed. It is essential for one's *spiritual formation that Christians grow in faith, hope, and love. The apostle Paul identified love as the greatest of these theological virtues.

vision of God. A metaphor for the immediate encounter with or revelation of God. In *Scripture, the prophets describe visions of God (Numbers 12:6; Ezekiel 1:1), and it was prophesied that the young would see visions (Joel 2:28; Acts 2:17). In Catholic tradition, the *beatific vision of God is considered the consummate *union (or communion) with the divine.

vivification. The term used especially by Reformed Christians to talk about the effectual work of God's *grace in sanctifying people, restoring them into the *image of God, in which people were created (e.g., John Calvin). Just as God effectually justifies those whom he elected for *salvation, God effectually vivifies them. Neither one is the result of human works, but both are gifts that God chooses to bestow. Christians are to give thanks and *praise to God as they experience this divinely given vivification. In response to God's vivification, Christians are to *mortify themselves in order to subdue remaining sin in their lives and society.

vocation. God's *calling of people, usually with regard to work on behalf of the church or ministry, but may also apply to secular work. Calling (Lat., *vocatio*) also has to do with the call of God to people for *salvation and for their spiritual well-being. But when talked about as a vocation, Christians may refer to a sense of spiritual calling to serve others, both in clergy and lay capacities.

volition. *See* freedom, human.

W

war, holy. War fought for religious reasons, considered a manifestation of spiritual *godliness. Some Christians believe wars may be fought for holy reasons, especially wars fought for religious goals; as such, they abide by a just war rationale, reminiscent of many wars commanded by God in the OT (e.g., Joshua, David). The medieval Crusades against Muslims in the eleventh to thirteenth centuries are examples of holy wars. Fighting in such wars is considered spiritually beneficial, though not all Christians consider every (or any) war justifiable. Indeed some Christians consider peacemaking and pacifism more spiritually beneficial, reminiscent of *Jesus' emphasis on peaceful resistance to violence (e.g., turning the other cheek, Matthew 5:39).

warfare, spiritual. *See* spiritual warfare.

water. In Christianity water signifies a number of religious and spiritual realities. Religiously, water is important throughout *Scripture, symbolizing life, *salvation, and ritualistic cleansing. Jesus talked about *salvation as "living water . . . a spring of water gushing up to eternal life" (John 4:10, 14). The *ritual use of water is especially important to Christians for the *sacrament of *baptism, involving the sprinkling of water or immersion of new believers in it. Spiritually, water is often used as an analogy of the cleansing and *purification God intends for Christians.

What would Jesus do? (or WWJD). The question asked by the characters in Charles Sheldon's nineteenth-century novel *In His Steps*, in order to encourage Christians to live more like Jesus Christ. Sheldon emphasized the need for Christians to emulate Jesus' care for the poor as well as for people's spiritual well-being. Although Sheldon asked the question with a social gospel emphasis in mind, it has been used by Christians as a challenge for *spiritual formation.

wilderness. An analogy used to describe spiritual barrenness or a time of spiritual dryness. In church history, some Christians lived ascetically in literal wilderness contexts for the benefit of their spiritual formation. *Jesus Christ had a wilderness experience in *Scripture in which he was *tempted by *Satan and overcame the physical and spiritual challenges he faced (Matthew 4:1-11). Christians may still describe their physical and spiritual challenges as a wilderness experience, believing that God will enable them to overcome their challenges.

will of God. God's intent for the world or *humanity in general as well as for individual people. *Scripture describes people as acting by the will of God (e.g., 1 Corinthians 1:1), and people are exhorted to discern the will of God (e.g., Romans 12:2). In Scripture, God's will is stated in many ways. For example, 1 Thessalonians 4:3 says: "For this is the will of God, your sanctification." In addition to Scripture, people seek God's will through *prayer, Christian writings, Christian counsel, and other *spiritual disciplines.

wine. When *Jesus Christ blessed and served wine to his *disciples during their last supper together, it became religiously significant for Christians. Wine then became ritualistically important in partaking of the *Eucharist (or *Lord's Supper, *Communion). Catholics believe that wine blessed for the Eucharist transubstantiates into the blood of Jesus. In commiseration with those who struggle with alcoholism, some church traditions sacramentally use grape juice rather than wine.

wisdom (or prudence). Perception, insight, or good judgment thought to exceed knowledge alone, considered invaluable for religious and spiritual well-being. Sometimes wisdom is thought to be a special human quality, for example, as found in Proverbs. As such, people are encouraged to grow in wisdom, and great wisdom is praised (Ephesians 5:15). However, human wisdom alone is thought to be limited (1 Corinthians 1:19). The greatest wisdom requires proper perspective of God (Proverbs 9:10) and is sometimes given by God (1 Kings 4:29). Thus wisdom contributes to Christian spirituality in many ways. In 1 Corinthians 12:8 Paul says that the Holy *Spirit gives to believers the utterance or gift of wisdom. Wisdom is also known as prudence, which is one of the four cardinal *virtues.

wisdom, gift of. A special enabling of the Holy *Spirit that empowers believers to be wise in the ways of God. Like all gifts, Christians may grow in their understanding and giving out of wisdom.

women's spirituality. Spirituality distinctive to women. There is no agreement among Christians with regard to whether there is spirituality distinctive to women, in contrast to men. But increasingly some emphasize the need to understand and promote spirituality among women differently than men, and vice versa. Women's spirituality may be complementarian or egalitarian in orientation. Biblical *feminists have especially identified gender needs and concerns among women with regard to their egalitarian understanding and spiritual development. For example, consideration is given to biological and cultural differences, including historic marginalization and oppression, which make women's experience of God, *salvation, and spirituality different from that of men. *See also* men's spirituality.

word of faith. A Pentecostal movement that emphasizes the power of faith. Christians are believed to have access to holistic *blessing (spiritual, physical, emotional, and financial) through speaking in faith, often called "*naming and claiming" or "promise claiming."

work. The labor one does, physically, mentally, and in other ways, which is considered complementary to one's spiritual well-being. Biblically, God created people to work (Genesis 2:15), and work is to be "done for the Lord" and not just for human needs (Colossians 3:23). After the fall of humanity into *sin, work became more difficult. But work may be a vocation for people, which leads to spiritual well-being as well as for providing for basic human needs. During the seventeenth century, Brother Lawrence developed his rule of work and spirituality that could be followed doing the most mundane of jobs. In both one's personal and professional work responsibilities, one's labor may aid in spiritual reflection on God and things related to God, which strengthen one's spirituality as well as one's work.

worship. The demonstration of *love, reverence, *adoration, and consecration toward God. Although it is most often thought of as a public practice, worship represents an inner attitude and relationship with God characterized by holy consecration to God (Romans 12:1). It is expressed in a variety of ways through personal or corporate acts, using liturgical or extemporaneous expressions of *praise and *thanksgiving. Worship is aided by attitudes of *humility, honesty, and *celebration of God, honoring God's attributes, character, and works. It may include the singing of *psalms, *hymns, and spiritual *songs to God (Colossians 3:16). Worship may serve as a spiritual discipline that enables people to focus on God and Christian devotion.

Z

Zion. The biblical name for a mountain near Jerusalem, or a name used for Jerusalem itself. Zion has been used to symbolize heaven, the "heavenly Jerusalem" (Hebrews 12:22), as well as to symbolize the church (Hebrews 12:23). It has repeatedly been used by Christians in talking and singing about their *hope of spiritual peace and flourishing, in this life, and for eternal life to come.

Pocket Reference Collection from IVP Academic

InterVarsity Press
Downers Grove, Illinois 60515
ivpress.com